THE
TOUGH KID
SOCIAL SKILLS
BOOK

Part of the "Tough Kid" Series by
Rhode, Jenson, & Reavis

Susan M. Sheridan, Ph.D.

Tough Kid illustrations by Tom Oling
Text layout and design by Susan Krische
Cover design by Londerville Design
Edited by Maureen Adams

ISBN 1-57035-051-5

Printed in the United States of America

Published and Distributed by

SOPRIS
WEST
4093 Specialty Place • Longmont, CO 80504 • (303) 651-2829
www.sopriswest.com

75SOCIAL/6-01/EDB/4M/307

Acknowledgments

I am greatly indebted to several people who have helped in the development of this book. First, I would like to recognize Dr. Bill Jenson for his inspiration and commitment to this project. He, Dr. Ginger Rhode, and Dr. Ken Reavis are responsible for the original "Tough Kid" book, and provided much encouragement and support. Second, I am indebted to Candace Dee, Dory Walker, Sondra Russman, Megan McCormick, Julie Morgan, and others who have worked with me on many social skills groups over the years. They have helped shape and add life to the program (and in the meantime, provided wonderful services to some very "Tough Kids!"). I also truly appreciate all of the students and their families who have been part of the Tough Kids social skills programs. These individuals worked very hard and showed outstanding commitment to making some changes in their lives. Finally, thanks are extended to the production staff at Sopris West for their assistance on this project.

Dedication

This book is dedicated to Jack and Carol Sheridan who, through their own examples, taught me the importance of friendship, kindness, and social skills.

Table of Contents

Introduction: What This Book Will Do For You 1

Part I—Social Skills Concepts

Chapter 1: Overview 5

How Do Tough Kids Differ From Other Kids?. 5

How Do Tough Kids Behave Socially?. 6

Excesses in Using Aggressive Behaviors. 6

Deficits in Following Rules, Using Self-Control, and Solving Problems 7

What Do Tough Kids Think About Friends? 7

How Are Tough Kids Perceived by Others? 8

Summary 9

Chapter 2: Assessing Social Skills 11

Multi-Gating Assessment Procedure 11

Step 1: General Screening 12

Step 2: Rating Scales 15

Step 3: Direct Assessment 18

Outcome of Social Skills Assessment 22

Summary 26

Chapter 2 Reproducibles 29

Tough Kid Teacher Nomination 31

Student Sociometric. 33

Skills Survey 35

Social Skills Interview 37

Student Social Skills Interview 39

Social Skills Direct Observation 41

Assessment Summary. 45

Chapter 3: Three Levels of Social Skills Training 47

Small Group Social Skills Training 47

Classroom-Based Social Skills Training 52

School-Wide Social Skills Training 56

Combining Approaches 60

Summary 62

Chapter 3 Reproducibles 63

Home-School Note 65

Weekly Social Skills Record 67

Self-Assessment for Group Sessions 69

Flying High With Social Skills 71

I Was Caught Doing a Super Job! 73

Classroom Bank Points 75

Chapter 4: Leading a Social Skills Group 77

Leader Skills 77

Group Procedures 78

Other Program Components 93

Generalization of Social Skills—Making It Count in the Real World 96

Working With Parents and Teachers 99

Summary 101

Chapter 4 Reproducibles 103

Social Situations for Role Play 105

Social Skills Contract 107

Weekly Contract 109

Homework Sheet 111

Weekly Homework Chart 113

Social Skills Homework Thermometer 115

Certificate 117

Group Rules 119

Part II—Training Session Outlines

Introduction 123

Target Skills 123

Opening Session 125

Skill Area A: Social Entry 127

Session 1
Subskill 1: Body Basics/Starting a Conversation 127

Session 2
Subskill 2: Joining In 130

Session 3
Subskill 3: Recognizing and Expressing Feelings 132

Skill Area B: Maintaining Interactions 135

Session 4
Subskill 4: Having a Conversation 135

Session 5
Subskill 5: Playing Cooperatively 137

Skill Area C: Problem Solving 141

Session 6
Subskill 6: Solving Problems 141

Session 7
Subskill 7: Using Self-Control 144

Session 8
Subskill 8: Solving Arguments 146

Session 9
Subskill 9: Dealing With Teasing 149

Session 10
Subskill 10: Dealing With Being Left Out 152

Session 11
Subskill 11: Accepting "No" 154

Last Session 157

Booster Session 159

Skill Sheets 167

Classroom Posters 191

References 219

What This Book Will Do For You

In *The Tough Kid Book: Practical Classroom Management Strategies* (Rhode, Jenson, & Reavis, 1992), a "Tough Kid" was defined as a student who displays excesses in noncompliance and aggression, and deficits in self-management, academic, and social skills. This book will focus on one of the primary deficit areas of Tough Kids: **social skills**. In it, specific methods to assess and teach Tough Kids appropriate social skills will be presented and reviewed in detail.

For the purposes of this book, social skills are defined as learned behaviors that are necessary to get along successfully in a majority of social situations. Unfortunately, Tough Kids often experience unsuccessful interactions and have a difficult time getting along in most situations, largely because they have not learned appropriate ways for behaving socially. Therefore, the premise of this book is that Tough Kids need to be taught appropriate social skills, just as they need to be taught academic or self-management skills.

This book is meant to help teachers, school psychologists, school counselors, school social workers, and other support staff implement social skills programs for Tough Kids. It will provide information on how to identify Tough Kids who are in need of direct social skills training. In addition, this book will suggest practical ways to assess important social skills, with reproducible forms and strategies to structure the data gathering process. Procedures for leading social skills groups, including forms, charts, and recommendations, are presented to provide users with practical information. Finally, step-by-step procedures are provided for conducting structured social skills programs in small group, classroom, or school-wide applications.

Part I, Social Skills Concepts, provides information to maximize the effectiveness of your social skills program. Chapter 1 presents an overview of the social problems of Tough Kids, as well as comparisons between children with and without friends. The importance of social skills training for the Tough Kid is emphasized. Chapter 2 describes a multi-gating assessment procedure that can help practitioners identify those students who are in the greatest need of structured social skills training. Procedures for conducting an evaluation, including teacher nominations, sociometrics, rating scales, interviews, and observations, are presented.

Information regarding various procedures for structuring social skills training begins in Chapter 3. In this chapter, three possible levels for intervention are described. These include small group, classroom-based, and school-wide social skills training. Suggestions for leading social skills groups are presented in Chapter 4. Also in Chapter 4 are specific tools and tactics for structuring social skills group interventions. The primary components include group discussion, modeling, role playing, providing feedback, setting up homework, and developing contracts. These procedures are common among many social skills curricula, such as *Skillstreaming the Elementary School Child* (1984) by McGinnis & Goldstein; however, they are presented here with particular attention to their usefulness in various group formats, and in relation to Tough Kids.

Part II of the book, Training Session Outlines, presents actual outlines that can be used when conducting social skills sessions of all sizes. The outlines cover skills in the general areas of social entry, maintaining interactions, and solving problems. The same procedures can be used whether you are conducting small group social skills sessions (three to eight students) or sessions in entire classrooms or schools. The outlines are structured to be completed in 60 minutes, but individual practitioners can modify the program in any way necessary to meet their students' needs and to accommodate school or work schedules.

SOCIAL

SKILLS

CONCEPTS

PART I

Chapter 1

Overview

Although many Tough Kids may say that friends do not matter, this is not true. Friends are extremely important in students' lives for many reasons. When interacting with others, students learn how to cooperate, compromise, make decisions, and solve problems. They engage each other to learn the importance of sharing, communicating, and helping. Groups of friends help students learn the importance of belonging to a group, develop a sense of identity, and figure out how to give and receive support. And knowing that one is liked by others can help students feel proud, worthwhile, and important. For some students, making friends is easy and natural; for others, such as Tough Kids, active efforts at teaching social skills are necessary to allow them to have meaningful relationships with peers and adults.

"Too Cool"

How Do Tough Kids Differ From Other Kids?

There are some important differences in the ways that Tough Kids act around other students that distinguishes them from the others. Perhaps a good place to start is by describing what socially able students do, or what behaviors are demonstrated by students who get along well with others.

Students who are well liked typically spend much of their day playing with friends. They will suggest playing more often, and will almost always agree when asked by a friend to play. They communicate clearly with others and check for clarification when they do not understand others (Doll, Sheridan, & Law, 1990).

Students with lots of friends usually treat their friends more kindly than do those with few friends. Compared to Tough Kids, they are likelier to say kind things and to share. You may see them sympathizing with a friend that is hurt, defending a friend that is being teased, helping a friend when

he/she needs assistance, and complimenting a friend.

All students will have disagreements when they interact with friends. Important differences between well-liked and unliked kids (such as Tough Kids), are apparent in how they settle their problems with friends. Socially able students can think of several alternatives to choose from when solving problems with friends. They are apt to suggest a compromise and may give up some of what they want to in order to maintain friendships. They will take the time to explain why they want to play a certain game, or use a certain rule. And they are likely to listen when a peer explains his/her side.

> **All students will have disagreements . . . .**

How Do Tough Kids Behave Socially?

When you think about the Tough Kids in your classroom or school, chances are you think about how they act that differentiates them from other students. It is usually not hard to pick out the Tough Kids based on their behaviors and the way they deal with problems. In most cases, Tough Kids use externalizing behaviors (behavioral excesses) in their interactions with others. From watching Tough Kids in peer groups, it is also clear that they have deficits in certain areas, as though they have not learned the necessary skills to handle situations in an effective manner. What are the **behavioral excesses** and **deficits** of Tough Kids?

Excesses in Using Aggressive Behaviors

The primary behavioral characteristic of Tough Kids is their aggressive style of dealing with others. They are often "in your face" and do not understand that there are more effective ways of solving problems.

When in a conflict, Tough Kids tend to lash out at others by shoving, pushing, hitting, kicking, or throwing objects.

"Gentle Persuasion"

How Do Tough Kids Behave With Others?

Tough Kids have important behavioral excesses and deficits that hinder their ability to get along well with others.

Behavioral Excesses:
- Aggression
- Arguing
- Hitting
- Fighting
- Shouting
- Teasing
- Blaming
- Provoking

Behavioral Deficits:
- Using self-control
- Cooperating
- Problem solving
- Helping
- Sharing
- Making good decisions
- Accepting "No"

They try to bully their way through situations by using forceful words and actions. If they have a disagreement they argue, whine, scream, or tantrum. Even in neutral or nonproblematic situations, Tough Kids usually end up in a negative encounter by trying to get their way or win at all costs. They do not play fairly and ignore the rights of other students. The bottom line is, Tough Kids are not fun to be around.

Deficits in Following Rules, Using Self-Control, and Solving Problems

The problems Tough Kids have with aggression stem partly from their difficulties following rules and using self-control. Tough Kids usually have not internalized social "rules" for behavior, such as how to have positive interactions and solve problems. This lack of an internal set of rules (values) about appropriate social behaviors is problematic, but becomes magnified when coupled with lack of self-control.

Tough Kids tend to be impulsive. They react immediately and often seem out of control in problematic situations. A classic behavior of Tough Kids is their inability to take ownership of or responsibility for their problems. You have probably had firsthand experience with this—Tough Kids usually blame other kids or act as though they had absolutely no control over their actions, problems, or situations. Often we have heard Tough Kids say: "It wasn't my fault!" or "I couldn't help it!"

"Establishing Rules"

Another deficit that Tough Kids have is in their problem-solving skills. In problem situations, Tough Kids tend to react without thinking and their solutions for problems tend to be aggressive or counterproductive. Take Bubba. Bubba wants to play tetherball at recess, but Sam wants to play kickball. Rather than considering options for solving the problem, such as compromising by playing kickball first and tetherball second,

Bubba argues and fights with Sam until Sam walks away and plays with Fred. Bubba is left alone, but continues to yell and scream at Sam as though by Bubba's doing so, Sam will come back and play.

The problem with Tough Kids' problem-solving abilities is that they rarely consider various ways of solving problems, and the consequences of these various actions. In most cases, they do not realize that there are several ways of getting what they want (e.g., playing tetherball), so the first thing that enters their minds (which is usually aggressive) is the response they tend to go with. They are deficient in using prosocial behaviors when dealing with other students, especially when there is a conflict.

What Do Tough Kids Think About Friends?

Tough Kids do not just behave differently than other students, they also think about situations, especially conflict or problem situations, differently. We have already discussed the fact that Tough Kids tend to blame others for their problems; well, it does not stop there. Many Tough Kids actually believe that when something bad happens to them, it is because other students wanted it, even willed it, to happen. They tend to believe that everyone else dislikes them and is "out to get them" one way or another. They do not typically think about how other students might be feeling or thinking. In fact, they are often unable to conceive of the perspective of other students.

Tough Kids have a hard time "reading" social situations and knowing how to act around others. Most people are able to interpret and understand facial cues, body language, and other subtle aspects of a situation and respond accordingly. Tough Kids, however, just do not "get it." For example, Bubba's mother is having a luncheon with her neighborhood friends and asks him to go to his cousin's house after school and stay there until her guests go home. When Bubba comes storming into the house with mud on his shoes and a stray dog at his side, he does not understand his mother's stern look of discontent and anger, and later exclaims, "How can you ground me?! All I did was come home, like you always tell me to!"

"What's the problem?"

We have already talked about Tough Kids' deficits at solving problems effectively. When asked to think about possible solutions to problems, such as being teased or left out of a game, they generally give only a few answers, and these tend to be aggressive or antisocial. In fact, they have a hard time coming up with positive, assertive, or cooperative alternatives at all. So asking Tough Kids why they hit another student on the playground often leads to a dead-end response. It is likely that they did not know of any other possible alternatives. Even when they know a "better" (socially appropriate) way to respond, their impulsiveness and failure to consider consequences of their actions often get in the way. In addition, Tough Kids will also blame another or claim ignorance when questioned about a problem, using statements such as, "He started it!" or "I don't know what happened!"

Another aspect of Tough Kids' "cognitive set" is their difficulty recognizing cause and effect

relationships. They do not recognize the effect their behaviors have on other kids and on social interactions. For example, Bubba is playing checkers with Stanley and tries to win the game by making an inappropriate move. When Stanley accuses Bubba of cheating and goes home early, Bubba exclaims "Stanley just quit and went home! He's such a cry-baby!" Bubba does not understand that his extra move on the checkerboard effectively ended the game, as well as a relatively positive play situation.

How Are Tough Kids Perceived by Others?

In any classroom, students can be classified into one of four groups: **popular**, **neglected**, **rejected**, and **controversial**. These classifications are made by asking all students in the class to list the names of classmates with whom they would like to work or play, and to list the names of those with whom they would not prefer to work or play. They can also be asked to name students on other dimensions, such as those who play cooperatively, share their things, or offer help.

Popular students are those who are highly rated or named frequently as those with whom others would like to play. **Neglected** students are somewhat forgotten; not many classmates report them as those with whom they would like to play, and not many report them as those with whom they would not like to play. **Controversial** students are in the middle; several students say they would like to play with them, but several say they would not like to play with them. **Rejected** students are not named by many as those with whom they would like to play or work, but named by many of their classmates as those with whom they would not play or work. Guess where Tough Kids fall in this classification? Yes, Tough Kids tend to become rejected by their peers; other students soon figure out that their interactions with Tough Kids are less than pleasant and begin to avoid them, leave them out, or otherwise choose not to play or work together.

Even when Tough Kids go to new groups, such as a new school, church, or neighborhood, they are soon rejected by peers.

All students, even Tough Kids, can and do learn a great deal about social situations and socially appropriate behaviors from each other. Unfortunately, the more Tough Kids become rejected from their peer group, the more time they spend in isolation, away from the learning and reinforcement attained in groups. This isolation keeps Tough Kids from forming meaningful peer relationships. The longer Tough Kids are rejected by peers, the more time they will spend in isolation and the more difficult it will be for them to learn the important skills they need to interact with others, make decisions, and solve problems. The perpetual cycle that Tough Kids get into with peers begins. This cycle needs to be addressed in order to help the Tough Kid succeed now and later in life.

As Tough Kids grow up and enter middle and high school settings, their relationships with others do not naturally improve. They continue to seek attention from others, but the social behaviors in which they engage often become more antisocial. For example, Bubba's rude and sarcastic comments toward his teacher may take the form of swearing coupled with physical force as he gets older. In elementary school he may have tripped or shoved other students to get his way; in high school he is likelier to become involved in fist fights or use threatening comments toward other students. Tough Kids also tend to seek each other out for friendships, imitate each other's actions, and reinforce each other's inappropriate social behaviors. The attention they receive from each other is typically quite powerful in sustaining negative or antisocial behaviors. Gang-like behaviors, such as carrying a knife or gun, wearing intimidating clothing, and painting graffiti on school or community property are characteristic of older Tough Kids.

Summary

Social skills are learned behaviors that are necessary for students to get along with others successfully in a majority of situations, including in the school and in the community. However, Tough Kids present all kinds of deficits in social skills. Compared to well-liked students, Tough Kids are less able to come up with positive and effective solutions to problems. Rather, they have limited abilities at making appropriate decisions and compromising. They tend to react impulsively and aggressively and often fail to recognize their own actions as contributing to difficulties they have with peers. Their social skill deficits are not corrected on their own over time; Tough Kids continue to have problems with friends into adolescence and adulthood. Therefore, it is extremely important to treat the social skills deficits of Tough Kids through a comprehensive intervention program.

In Chapter 2, we will discuss methods to assess the social skills of elementary-aged Tough Kids, as well as what to do with the information collected. Then, a three-step model of social skills training will be described to allow you to introduce social skills training in small groups, classroom settings, or throughout the entire school building. Actual outlines presented later in this book will help you implement social skills programs at any one of these levels.

Assessing Social Skills

You may think that assessing Tough Kids' social skills is an unnecessary, time-consuming task. After all, these students seem to have **no skills to assess**! But a structured and semi-formal assessment procedure is actually quite important for several reasons. First, a comprehensive assessment approach will help you identify those Tough Kids who are in need of social skills training. Second, assessment will allow you to determine whether or not students have some important basic skills upon which they can build more complex skills. Third, a thorough assessment may assist in the selection of specific skill areas that need to be the target of the social skills intervention. Finally, assessment will allow teachers, school psychologists, or other staff to document actual student gains that are made during social skills training and beyond. As you can see, assessment is a vital first component of a total social skills intervention program.

Multi-Gating Assessment Procedure

There are many assessment techniques and methods available. In social skills work, however, it is important to collect information that is reliable (it is dependable), valid (it measures social skills and not some unrelated concept such as basket weaving), efficient (it does not cost a lot of time or money), and relevant (it has meaning) to the group or situation in which the students are involved. A multi-gating assessment procedure is recommended when assessing social skills. This type of assessment approach allows educators to collect broad-based information about individual and group needs, as well as systematically obtain specific and focused information about students.

Multi-gating assessments follow a **top-down** framework for collecting information (Walker, Severson, Stiller, Williams, Haring, Shinn, & Todis, 1988). A three-step assessment approach should be sufficient in identifying those Tough Kids who are in the greatest need of social skills training (Jones, Sheridan, & Binns, 1993). This approach will also enable you to notice specific skills in which they need instruction. The procedure suggested in this book involves three steps, and assessment at each step requires you to obtain information from more than one source in order to obtain various perspectives of each Tough Kid's social difficulties. For example, at Step 1, information is obtained from teachers and peers; at Step 2, adults and the student provide ratings; and Step 3 requires interviews with various people in several settings, such as classrooms, playgrounds, and homes.

Multi-gating assessments generally start with a quick and easy technique that requires broad-based information, and provides an initial assessment of Tough Kids' social behaviors and abilities. Examples of such measures include nominations and sociometric procedures. These procedures are cost- and time-efficient, and are helpful at narrowing in on the specific students who are in the greatest need of social skills training. For example, Ms. Snow lists the names of five students in her class who get into the most fights with other students. She also asks all of her fourth grade students to name their three best friends.

At the second step of screening, the assessment becomes more focused and requires more time to complete. Although they are slightly more time-consuming, assessment procedures at this step provide important information about specific concerns of teachers, parents, students, and others who know the target students well. At this step of assessment, you may begin to **pinpoint** (explicitly identify) some behavioral excesses (such as verbal outbursts or physical shoving) that need to decrease, and some prosocial skills (such as self-control and solving problems assertively) that Tough Kids need to learn. Some examples of assessment methods utilized at this stage include behavioral checklists and rating scales.

Finally, at the third step of assessment, specific and detailed information about social behaviors and problems of Tough Kids is attained. At this step of assessment it is also helpful to begin to look for environmental conditions related to the behavior in question, such as antecedents (things that come before), consequences (what comes after), and any patterns that may emerge. For example, you might notice that Bubba's verbal outbursts in the classroom are especially severe in the early afternoon immediately after lunch recess, late in the week, and following playground disagreements with Stanley and Myron. In this case, several environmental conditions, such as antecedent events, time of day, day of week, and peers present, seem to predict Bubba displaying a negative social behavior or verbal outburst. Some assessment techniques that can be used at this third assessment step include interviews with parents, teachers, playground monitors, and others who know Bubba well. Direct observations of Bubba's social skills in areas of the greatest concern are also useful, whenever possible (such as the playground or lunchroom).

This overview of multi-gating procedures should have provided you with a general understanding of the various methods and approaches used to assess social skills. Next, we will examine in detail the techniques used at each step of assessment. Keep in mind that you must select assessment methods that are appropriate and relevant for your situation. For example, if you are working in a school full of Tough Kids and want to implement a school-wide social skills program, assessment may stop after the collection of sociometric and rating scale data. This will allow you to identify the **toughest Tough Kids** in your school, do some evaluation prior to and after social skills training, and still get by in a cost-effective manner. On the other hand, if you wish to identify only a small subset of students in a grade or school who are in need of social skills training and you plan to provide their instruction in a small group, more comprehensive information will be necessary to select the social skills that are most important and relevant to the group. More in-depth information about the various ways that social skills instruction can be delivered is provided in Chapter 3.

Step 1: General Screening

There are two general methods of assessment at Step 1: **teacher nominations** and **sociometrics**. One of these is adult-focused, the other is peer-focused. This step is broad and general. The objective of this assessment step is to begin to identify those students who are being recognized by teachers and peers as having great difficulty getting along with others. Specific recommendations for completing this assessment step are in How To Box 2-1.

Teacher Nominations

Teacher nominations are quick, easy-to-collect methods of gathering information. They are useful to begin identifying students who are at the greatest risk for becoming Tough Kids. Also, there is usually a high correspondence between teacher

Recommendations for Completing Assessment Step 1

Nominations:

1. Send fliers to all teachers in the school, including resource, bilingual, and Chapter One teachers. Introduce yourself and your intent to conduct social skills training for Tough Kids. Ask for their cooperation in identifying students who can benefit from this training.

2. Define the type of student who is expected to benefit from the program. A sample definition might be: Students who have difficulties making and keeping friends. They argue, fight, blame others for problems, and are not well-liked by others. They have problems solving disagreements, using self-control, playing cooperatively, and staying out of fights.

3. Provide teachers with a form on which they can list no more than five students in their classroom who are similar to the type of student you described.

Sociometrics:

4. If teachers agree, go into their classrooms and conduct the sociometric assessments yourself. Explain to the class that you are interested in students' friendships.

5. Pass out sociometric forms that list the nomination criteria on the top. Both positive and negative nominations should be made.

6. Remind students that their nominations are strictly confidential (you do not want their names on the paper, and you will not be sharing their nominations with anyone). Also remind them not to talk about their nominations with anyone else.

7. Collect the sociometric forms and tally the number of times each student is nominated for a positive or negative response.

8. Rank order the class from highest to lowest in terms of their positive nominations and negative nominations. Those who have the fewest positive nominations and the most negative nominations are considered "rejected" (Tough Kids).

9. Compare the list of teacher nominations with the list of rejected students. If a student's name appears on both lists, he/she may be considered for the next step of assessment (Step 2).

10. Thank the teacher and the class for their help at this assessment step.

nominations and other information pointing to problem areas, suggesting that teachers know their students well!

A sample nomination form is included in Figure 2-1. When using nomination techniques, you can simply ask teachers to nominate the top five students in their class who have difficulty getting along with others, have few friends, or act aggressively with peers. In fact, you can ask for nominations based on any criteria for which you would like to select students for social skills training. This flexibility in the use of nomination techniques makes them very practical and meaningful. When using nominations, it is suggested

Figure 2-1

**Tough Kid
Teacher Nomination**

Teacher's Name: _____ Grade: _____

A social skills treatment program will be offered for students in this school. The students who are expected to benefit most from the program are those who:

    Have few friends
    Frequently fight or argue with classmates
    Blame others for problems that arise
    Do not show an ability to solve problems with classmates
    Fail to use self-control
    Are not well liked by others

You know the students in your classroom better than anyone! So, I would appreciate it if you could take a few minutes to think about your class and list on the lines below no more than five students who have difficulties such as the ones listed above. Once I have received your nominations, I will follow up with you regarding the next step of assessment. Thank you!

    1. _____
    2. _____
    3. _____
    4. _____
    5. _____

© 1995 by Sheridan, S.M. Available from Sopris West: Longmont, CO. (800) 547-6747
Part I—Social Skills Concepts

---

that you: (1) limit the number of nominations to no more than five from any classroom; and (2) develop specific criteria for nominations, rather than use nonspecific criteria such as, "Who should be in social skills groups?" These criteria should be related to the goals of the social skills program, as well as what you hope to include in training.

Sociometrics

Sociometric methods are used to obtain information from Tough Kids' peers. It is important to obtain an understanding of how students are perceived by their peers, and sociometrics can provide this information. After all, who better than classmates to give information on how Tough Kids behave in social situations?

Sociometrics are similar to teacher nominations, except that classmates are now the ones nominating each other. An example of a sociometric form is presented in Figure 2-2. As with teacher nominations, sociometrics are simple and quick to administer. Sociometrics work in the following fashion: each child in a classroom is asked to nominate three peers with whom they like to play or work, and three peers with whom they would not like to play or work. (You can also use other examples or activities, such as "Name three classmates you would invite to your birthday party," or "List three classmates with whom you would not eat lunch.") Class rosters might be passed out and students could be asked to "Circle the names of three classmates you would most/least want to invite to play." In the early

"Guess Who Belongs?"

elementary grades (first and second grades), you may use class pictures and have students mark with colored pens the photos of classmates they nominate.

Figure 2-2

Student Sociometric

On the lines below, you will be asked to name some classmates. The reason you are being asked to do this is to learn more about children's friendships. Please do not put your name on this paper. Your answers will not be known by anyone. Please do not tell anyone how you answered, and do not talk about this activity with your classmates once you have finished. Thank you!

1. List the names of three classmates with whom you like to play:

2. List the names of three classmates with whom you do **not** like to play:

3. List the names of three classmates whom you would invite to your birthday party:

4. List the names of three classmates whom you would **not** invite to a birthday party:

© 1995 by Sheridan, S.M. Available from Sopris West: Longmont, CO. (800) 547-6747
Part I—Social Skills Concepts

Based on the sociometric assessment results, students are classified as **popular**, **rejected**, **neglected**, or **controversial**. As we mentioned in Chapter 1, popular students are those who are nominated as fun to play with by several other students, and not nominated as someone with whom others would not like to play. Neglected students seem to be forgotten; they do not receive many nominations in either the positive or negative direction. Controversial students are those who fall somewhere in the middle; they receive some nominations in each category. Finally, rejected children, such as Tough Kids, are named frequently as those with whom classmates would not like to play, and rarely as those with whom they would like to play. For screening purposes, students who are nominated by their teachers as in need of social skills

assistance and by their peers as rejected, should be considered for the next step of assessment.

Step 2: Rating Scales

At Step 2, assessment activities are in the form of behavioral checklists and rating scales. It is important to remember that such information should be collected from various persons with whom each Tough Kid has contact. Although teacher-related checklists may be the easiest to obtain, they are only one aspect of assessment at this step. Ratings from parents and the students themselves should also be collected. Also, it is useful to use rating scales that assess general social skills as well as a scale that is very specific to the behaviors that the training program may address.

General Social Skills Rating Scales

There are many rating scales available for assessing the social skills of Tough Kids. A list of some scales and their general characteristics is presented in Box 2-1. Other rating scales and behavioral checklists are available that tap a range of problem areas (including social skills, but also a broader spectrum of problem areas, such as anxiety or depression).

If a general social skills rating scale (such as those in Box 2-1) is used, it is recommended that it be used only in conjunction with scales assessing specific social skills. This is because general scales do not achieve a necessary level of specificity for selecting target skills. They also do not always show sensitivity to treatments (i.e., even if Tough Kids make progress during social skills training, it may not show up on some broad scales of students' functioning).

Rating scales are used to assess the social skills of Tough Kids for a number of reasons. They are helpful in pinpointing students' social skills problems by asking about specific behaviors of the Tough Kids (such as their abilities to play cooperatively with others, accept criticism, or give compliments). They also provide an estimate of

Box 2-1

Brief Review of Social Skills Rating Scales

Social Skills Rating Scale (SSRS)
by Frank Gresham and Stephen Elliott
Published in 1990 by American Guidance Services - Circle Pines, MN.

- Preschool-grade 12 (separate forms are available for preschool, elementary, and secondary students).
- Forms available for parent, teacher, and student respondents, with 52, 53, and 39 items, respectively.
- Three major scales: Social Skills, Problem Behaviors, and Academic Competence.
- Social Skills factors include: Cooperation, Assertion, Self-Control, Responsibility, and Empathy on various forms.
- Problem Behaviors subscales include: Externalizing, Internalizing, Hyperactivity.
- Responses are made on a three-point Likert scale, with parent and teacher ratings for both frequency and importance of social behaviors.
- Normative sample adequate; reliability coefficients strong; evidence of content, criterion-related, and construct validity.

Walker-McConnell Scale of Social Competence
by Hill Walker and Scott McConnell
Published in 1988 by Pro-Ed - Austin, TX.

- Grades K-6.
- Teacher responds to 43 items on a five-point Likert scale.
- One major scale: Social Competence; three subscales: Teacher-Preferred Social Behavior, Peer-Preferred Social Behavior, and School Adjustment.
- Normative sample adequate; reliability data strong; evidence of construct and criterion-related validity.

School Social Behavior Scales (SSBS)
by Ken Merrell
Published in 1993 by Pro-Ed - Austin, TX.

- Grades K-12.
- Teachers respond to 65 items on a five-point Likert scale.
- Two major scales: Social Competence and Antisocial Behavior.
- Social Competence subscales include: Interpersonal Skills, Self-Management, Academic Skills; Antisocial Behavior subscales include: Hostile-Irritable, Antisocial-Aggressive, Disruptive-Demanding.

the severity of problems, such as how often problem behaviors (like arguing or fighting) occur. Rating scales can also provide a helpful guideline for questions to ask during interviews, and behaviors to look for in direct observations.

Of all the social skills scales now available, the *Social Skills Rating System* by Frank Gresham and Stephen Elliott is one of the best researched. There are separate *SSRS* forms for parents, teachers, and students that provide important information across raters (individuals) and settings (home, school, community). There are also separate forms to assess preschool, elementary, and secondary students. In general, the *SSRS* teacher form measures social skills in the areas of cooperation, assertion, and self-control. The parent and student forms assess these same types of skills, plus responsibility measured on the parent form and empathy assessed on the student form. A scale that measures "problem behaviors" is also included on the parent and teacher forms to assess problems associated with externalizing and internalizing disorders and hyperactivity. In addition, the teacher form assesses the student's academic competence. There is ample evidence of reliability and validity, suggesting that the data obtained through ratings on the *SSRS* will be accurate and meaningful.

The *SSRS* provides important information about social behaviors in terms of frequency (how often) and importance (how critical). Items are worded in a positive manner, so the scale is particularly effective at assessing social deficits. Also, behaviors assessed on the *SSRS* are stated in very specific terms, which is useful for developing goals and objectives for social skills training. For example, items on the *SSRS* ask parents, teachers, and students to rate how often the target student asks others to play and how often he/she solves arguments calmly. If respondents all agree that the student never completes these tasks, it can be inferred that he/she has a deficit in these skills, which would be a likely target for social skills intervention.

Standard scores are obtained based on the responses across all items on each scale (parent, teacher, student). The average standard score on the *SSRS* is 100; 67% of all students score between 85 and 115 and 99% score between 70 and 130. In general, Tough Kids obtain scores less than 70, estimating their social skills to be less developed than 98% of other students their age. This comparison to a normal group of peers, determined by scores obtained on the *SSRS* or other social skills rating scales, allows teachers and other school personnel to determine the severity of Tough Kids' social problems.

Specific Social Skills Rating Scales

In many cases, such as when entire classrooms or schools participate in social skills training, it will be impossible for teachers to complete comprehensive rating scales for each student in their classes. Therefore, abbreviated rating scales are available that ask for teachers' opinions about Tough Kids' social skills. One example is provided in Figure 2-3. The *Skills Survey* targets problems most concerning to parents and teachers of Tough Kids. This rating scale can be used both to prioritize skills to target for social skills training and to assess each student's ability to perform each skill. It can also be used as a measure of how well Tough Kids respond to efforts

Figure 2-3

Skills Survey

Student's Name: _____   Date: _____

Age: _____

The goal of the Social Skills Group is to identify specific areas in which students are experiencing difficulties, as well as to teach them positive social skills and behaviors in these problem areas. The behaviors listed below are several possible skill areas that may be targeted in the group. Your responses on this form will help us to identify areas that are problematic for students, and will assist in selecting specific skills to cover each week.

Using the scale of 1-4 listed below, please rate the degree to which each skill is a problem for the student. Thank you for your help.

1 - Never a problem
2 - Sometimes a problem
3 - Usually a problem
4 - Almost always a problem

Noticing and Talking About Feelings	1	2	3	4
Starting a Conversation	1	2	3	4
Joining In	1	2	3	4
Playing Cooperatively	1	2	3	4
Keeping a Conversation Going	1	2	3	4
Solving Problems	1	2	3	4
Solving Arguments	1	2	3	4
Dealing With Teasing	1	2	3	4
Dealing With Being Left Out	1	2	3	4
Using Self-Control	1	2	3	4
Accepting "No"	1	2	3	4

© 1995 by Sheridan, S.M. Available from Sopris West: Longmont, CO. (800) 547-6747
Part I—Social Skills Concepts

to teach them the specific skills outlined on the form.

The use of adult rating scales in the assessment of Tough Kids' social skills is based on the assumption that adults who know the students well are able to interpret and understand their social interactions with peers, in the social context in which they occur. But a large portion of the peer culture is not accessible or available to adults; therefore, adults' assessments may be biased by students' academic performances or behaviors towards adults. As a result, self-ratings and peer ratings (like sociometrics) are important.

Self-ratings provide very useful and interesting information about how students think about their own social skills; that is, how they behave and how others feel about them. Keep in mind that many Tough Kids deny their difficulties, fail to recognize their problems with peers, or respond in a way that they think you want them to. Others might overreport their problems. Still others are fairly accurate in noticing areas that are difficult

for them and how they differ from other students. Even though you may question the accuracy of some self-report assessment results, it is still useful to collect information about Tough Kids' self-perceptions before beginning social skills training in order to determine how their thoughts change over time. A step-by-step procedure for the use of rating scales is included in How To Box 2-2.

Step 3: Direct Assessment

Step 3 of the assessment is the most costly in terms of time and resources, but it derives the most direct and relevant information regarding Tough Kids' social skills and behaviors. Therefore, it is essential that you use the techniques described here whenever possible, particularly when small group interventions are used to teach social skills. You will find that the wealth of information you will receive is worth the time and effort!

Social Skills Interviews

Social skills interviews with parents, teachers, students, peers, and others such as lunchroom aides or playground staff are helpful in assessing the social problems of Tough Kids. Interviews will allow you to follow up on some information that you obtained previously through rating scales. A *Social Skills Interview* form for interviewing Tough Kids' parents and teachers is shown in Figure 2-4. Steps for conducting interviews are in How To Box 2-3.

Social skills interviews provide parents and teachers with ideas for those behaviors that are most important for a student to be successful in school and at home. They also allow you to begin to target specific skills for instruction. For example, Bubba's mother and teacher may both state that he has problems with accepting "No," thinking before blurting out a response, and joining into ongoing games appropriately. They may or may not agree on how important each skill is for getting along in their respective settings, but at

Figure 2-4

Social Skills Interview

Student's Name: _____ Date: _____
Teacher's Name: _____ Grade: _____
Parent's Name: _____ Date of Birth: _____

1. What are the specific concerns you have about _____'s social skills?

2. Which of these is the most problematic?

3. How often does it occur and how long has it been a problem?

4. Where does it occur?

5. What happens before the problem behavior?

6. What happens after the problem behavior?

7. What school or classroom procedures or rules are in place?

8. What do you expect of the student? What would be a reasonable goal for him/her?

9. What are some things the student excels at? What is his/her strengths? What does he/she like?

10. How and when can the problem be observed? How can data be collected on the problem?

How To Box 2-2

Suggestions for Using Rating Scales

1. Obtain consent from parents before completing or asking others to complete any rating scale.

2. Collect rating scale information from teachers, parents, and students. If possible, use a rating scale that has comparable forms for each respondent. When the students have more than one teacher, collect the information from all teachers who know the student well.

3. Explain the purpose of the rating scale and the procedures for completing it to the respondents before you give it to them. Show them the scale and describe how responses are made. Ask them to respond to each item, to provide only one rating per item, and to use only the choices given (for example, do not provide half-point responses). Assure them that the responses will be kept confidential.

4. Score the rating scales carefully. Make sure you use the correct tables to transfer the raw score (the score you get from adding the respondent's scores) to the standard score. Separate tables are often provided for age, grade, and gender. Some scales also have separate tables for students who are disabled and those who are not. You can use either scale, depending on the group with which you want to compare each student.

5. Double-check everything! (This includes student's name and birthdate, your addition, the transfer of scores to tables, and reference to standard score tables.)

6. If you are using the rating scale as a posttest measure of changes students made after social skills training, ask the respondent to think of the last two weeks and make responses based on students' behaviors in that time frame.

7. Thank teachers, parents, or students for completing the scales honestly.

least they have provided you with important information on skill areas that represent deficits for Bubba. It is likely that if you interviewed the playground aide, he/she would report that these behaviors are extremely important during recess and would support all efforts at teaching Bubba these skills! We will discuss more about the importance of support staff in the generalization section of Chapter 4.

Whenever possible, it is important to interview the students who will be receiving social skills training. You may think it sounds peculiar to consider "interviewing" students, but it is essential that students' thoughts about their problems are taken into consideration. This includes asking students what types of problems they have with friends, what they would like to see happen regarding friendships, and ideas they have about developing friendships. This information will be invaluable in helping you determine the Tough Kids' ownership of problems (Do they acknowledge their own problems, or do they blame others for them?); ability to set social goals for themselves (Do they have realistic or unrealistic expectations about themselves, their abilities, and their friends?); and knowledge of appropriate strategies they can use to make their social relationships better (Are they able to think about several solutions to problems, or just one? Do they recognize the consequences of their choices?). A *Student Social Skills Interview* form is presented in Figure 2-5.

How To Box 2-3

Steps for Conducting Social Skills Interviews

1. Invite the parents and teachers to participate in the interview together. This helps gather a great deal of information about concerns that each has about the Tough Kid's social skills, as well as to identify similarities and differences in their concerns.

2. Follow a structured interview guide to keep your discussion focused on parents' and teachers' concerns. The form presented in Figure 2-4 may be useful.

3. Use open-ended questions to begin the interview. These are questions that cannot be answered with a simple yes or no response. They invite a lengthy response and are useful for obtaining a great deal of information about the primary concerns. For example, you might start the interview with a statement such as "Tell me about your concerns about Bubba's social skills." Other open-ended questions might start with "How . . . ?"; "Why . . . ?"; and "What . . . ?"

4. Follow open-ended questions with requests for more information or examples. Try to get specific information about the Tough Kid's social deficits. Good questions for gathering more information often start with, "Explain what you mean . . . ," "Give me some examples . . . ," and "Tell me more about that . . . ."

5. Frequently check for your understanding of the parents' and teachers' concerns. Summarize what they are telling you and ask them if your summaries are accurate.

6. Keep the interview focused on specific **behaviors** that the Tough Kid is showing, rather than allowing the teacher or parent to focus on his/her personality or temperament. For example, a statement such as "He's just obnoxious!" may portray an accurate account of how the teacher is feeling about Bubba, but it does not tell you exactly what Bubba does that is bothersome. A better, more specific statement such as "He pesters the other students by poking and teasing them," will help you establish more appropriate treatment decisions.

7. Ask about events or situations that come before and after the Tough Kid displays inappropriate social behaviors. The events or situations that you might explore are numerous. For example, you might ask who is present, the time of day, and what is going on in the setting when Bubba shows difficulties. For instance, he might be teased or provoked by an older bully on the playground, someone might tell him to do an unpleasant task, or there may be little structure or supervision in the setting when he has problems with peers.

8. Assess the parents' and teachers' expectations of the Tough Kid by asking what they would like to see him/her doing; in other words, what might be a goal for Bubba? Ask them about other students in the classroom.

9. Plan to follow the interview with some of your own observations of Bubba on the playground, in the classroom, or in any other setting that may be problematic.

10. Thank the parents and teachers for their time. Give them your phone number or an easy way for them to contact you if they think of anything else that might be important.

Direct Observations

Direct observations provide a direct measurement of students' social interactions in real settings such as the classroom, playground, and hallways. Although direct observations can be quite time-consuming, they give firsthand information that cannot be collected in any other way. For example, direct observations in the lunchroom will allow you to notice things occurring there that may be affecting a Tough Kid's problems in that setting. These observations also provide an opportunity to view the behaviors and reactions of Tough Kids' peers, which is especially important in social skills programs.

There are at least two additional reasons why direct observations are important. First, they allow you to compare the Tough Kids' behaviors with those of other students in the same situation or setting. This is useful to see firsthand how Tough Kids differ from other students. Second, if you can observe Tough Kids once or twice a week during social skills training, you will be able to

"Who's Observing Who?"

determine how they are responding to the program (i.e., whether there are any real changes in their behaviors), and how effective the social skills training is at teaching them to use important social skills.

It is important to observe Tough Kids in as many different social settings as possible. This is because, as you have probably recognized, students do not act the same way in all places. Also, they do not react similarly when they are engaged in different tasks. For example, in the classroom when the principal steps in, Bubba might use a phrase such as "Excuse me, Penelope, can I please borrow your scissors?" Yet, on the playground with no authority figures around, he might say something such as "Gimme the soccer ball now, dude, before I nail you!" It is important to understand how Tough Kids' behaviors vary in different situations, when a variety of individuals and tasks are present.

An easy to use *Social Skills Direct Observation* form is shown in Figure 2-6. On the form, each of the general social skills categories that are taught to Tough Kids in this program is defined and measured. The three general categories are: (1) social entry/initiation, (2) maintaining interactions/playing cooperatively, and (3) solving problems/using self-control. A simple **partial interval** procedure is used. This requires you to observe the student for 15 seconds. At the end of

Figure 2-5

Student Social Skills Interview

Student's Name: _____ Date: _____

Teacher's Name: _____ Grade: _____

Parent's Name: _____ Date of Birth: _____

1. Tell me about yourself. What do you like to do?

2. Tell me about your friends. How many do you have? Who is your best friend? What do you like to do with your friends?

3. What do you want to happen when you play with friends? What usually happens?

4. Everyone has problems once in a while with their friends. What kinds of problems do you have with your friends? Tell me about the last time you had a problem with a friend.

5. How do you usually solve your problems with friends? How did you solve the last problem you had with a friend?

6. Are there other ways that you could have solved the problem? (List the solutions provided by the student.)

   Solutions:
   6a._____
   6b._____
   6c._____
   6d._____
   6e._____

7. Looking at the list, what might happen if you did each of the things you just mentioned? (List the consequences provided by the student.)

   Consequences:
   7a._____
   7b._____
   7c._____
   7d._____
   7e._____

8. Are friends important? Why or why not?

9. If you could change one thing about yourself or your friendships, what would it be?

© 1995 by Sheridan, S.M. Available from Sopris West: Longmont, CO. (800) 547-6747
Part I—Social Skills Concepts

Figure 2-6

Social Skills Direct Observation

Student's Name: _____ Date: _____
Setting: _____ Grade: _____

		A (15 seconds)	B (30 seconds)	C (45 seconds)	D (60 seconds)
1	S+	SE PC SP	SE PC SP	SE PC SP	SE PC SP
	S-	VA PA SN IS	VA PA SN IS	VA PA SN IS	VA PA SN IS
2	S+	SE PC SP	SE PC SP	SE PC SP	SE PC SP
	S-	VA PA SN IS	VA PA SN IS	VA PA SN IS	VA PA SN IS
3	S+	SE PC SP	SE PC SP	SE PC SP	SE PC SP
	S-	VA PA SN IS	VA PA SN IS	VA PA SN IS	VA PA SN IS
4	S+	SE PC SP	SE PC SP	SE PC SP	SE PC SP
	S-	VA PA SN IS	VA PA SN IS	VA PA SN IS	VA PA SN IS
5	S+	SE PC SP	SE PC SP	SE PC SP	SE PC SP
	S-	VA PA SN IS	VA PA SN IS	VA PA SN IS	VA PA SN IS
6	S+	SE PC SP	SE PC SP	SE PC SP	SE PC SP
	S-	VA PA SN IS	VA PA SN IS	VA PA SN IS	VA PA SN IS

Summary Table

Count the total number of slashes made for each behavior. Record the totals on the lines below.
Divide the number of intervals observed and report the rate for each behavior.

		Total	#Intervals	Rate			Total	#Intervals	Rate
S+:	SE	____	/ ____	=	S-:	VA	____	/ ____	=
	PC	____	/ ____	=		PA	____	/ ____	=
	SP	____	/ ____	=		SN	____	/ ____	=
						IS	____	/ ____	=

© 1995 by Sheridan, S.M. Available from Sopris West: Longmont, CO. (800) 547-6747
Part I—Social Skills Concepts

each 15-second interval, indicate with a slash each behavior you saw him/her demonstrate during that time. After 20 minutes, take out a new observation sheet and observe another student of the same sex who is not experiencing significant social problems (but do not select the most popular student in the group). Observe this comparison student using the same procedures for 20 minutes to get a sense of how a particular Tough Kid fares in comparison to others in his/her social circle. Instructions for using the *Social Skills Direct Observation* form are included in How To Box 2-4. Definitions for the behavior codes are in Box 2-2.

Outcome of Social Skills Assessment

Based on the assessment information, you should be able to do at least three things. First, you should be able to identify the students in your school who are most in need of social skills treatment (in other words, the "toughest Tough Kids"). Second, you should be able to identify specific social behaviors that are most problematic for Tough Kids, which will then be targeted in a social skills treatment program. Finally, you should be able to determine whether the Tough Kids have skill or performance deficits.

Identifying Students for Social Skills Treatment

An important piece of information that you will obtain through the multi-gating assessment approach is the identification of students in your school who are in greatest need of social skills treatment. A flowchart for assessment, with the outcome being selection of students for a small group social skills program, is presented in Figure 2-7 on page 25. At each step of the assessment process, you will be asking questions similar to those in the flowchart regarding the appropriateness of including individual students in a social skills treatment program. If you follow the guidelines suggested in the flowchart, combined with your own good judgment, you will have identified a group of students in need of social skills training and will be almost ready to start a treatment program!

Selecting Skills to Teach

It is important to decide the specific behaviors that are to be taught in your social skills program. This decision should be based on the assessment information you obtained and the collective needs or problems shown by students who will be participating in the social skills training. In general, deficits can be in the areas of social entry, maintaining interactions, or solving problems/using self-control. Examples of specific skills within each of those areas are in Box 2-3 on page 25. Guidelines for deciding which skills to teach are in How To Box 2-5 on page 26.

How To Box 2-4

Instructions for Conducting Direct Observations

1. Study the behavioral definitions in Box 2-2 carefully before beginning the observation. Use only the definitions provided for the observation to avoid confusion. Make sure that you use the same definitions for each observation.

2. Start your stopwatch at the **beginning** of the first interval. Begin observing. Observe the student for 15 seconds.

3. At the end of the 15-second interval, record the behaviors you observed with a slash through the appropriate code. Record the behavior if it occurred at all. Use the codes in the first (top left) cell only for the first 15-second interval. Allow your stopwatch to continue running.

4. Score the behaviors quickly and begin observing again for another 15-second interval. When your stopwatch indicates :30, record your observations in the box to the right of the previous recording. In other words, record your observations from left to right as time elapses.

5. More than one behavior can be recorded per interval, but each behavior should be recorded only once during each interval. For example, if you see the target student ask two different students to play and then yell at one of them when he is turned down, SE and VA would each be scored once for the interval.

6. Columns on the *Social Skills Direct Observation* form indicate the **end** of the point at which you should record students' behaviors.

7. Rows on the observation form indicate the minutes elapsed in the observation. Because each column represents 15 seconds, one minute will have elapsed when you complete the first row.

8. Summarize the data by adding the total number of slashes recorded for each behavior. Complete the summary table by recording totals and dividing each total by the number of intervals. This will give you a rate for each behavior exhibited by the student. As observations occur over time, these behavior rates can be comared to each other to gauge the Tough Kid's progress.

Determining Skill and Performance Deficits

Another important outcome of social skills assessment is identifying whether Tough Kids have skill or performance deficits. **Skill deficits** are demonstrated when the information obtained from assessments suggest that the Tough Kid clearly does not know how to perform a skill. For example, you may observe that Bubba virtually never solves arguments with his peers calmly; he raises his voice, blames the other kids for problems, and calls them names. If Bubba's parents and teachers report a similar sequence of events, you might assume that he lacks the basic knowledge of **how to** solve arguments calmly. If this is the case, you will need to do some direct teaching of this skill (solving arguments) during social skills training. Direct teaching can be accomplished by combining instruction, modeling, coaching, and cognitive problem-solving strategies.

Performance deficits are seen when the assessment information suggests that Tough Kids know how to perform the skill because they do it once in a while, but they do not perform it on a

Box 2-2

Definitions for Direct Observation Codes

Positive Social Behaviors (S+)

Social Entry (SE): Student spontaneously: (a) makes a statement or gesture clearly requesting another to engage in a mutual activity or conversation, or (b) enters an ongoing conversation or activity with another individual successfully, without being prompted, and in a socially appropriate way (i.e., without interrupting, raising voice, or using physical force). Examples include approaching a peer and asking him/her to play a game, asking a peer a question, waving to a friend to come over, and asking to join an ongoing game.

Playing Cooperatively (PC): Student appropriately keeps an interaction going, evidenced by prosocial behaviors such as sharing, helping, taking turns, cooperating, and engaging in positive conversation. Examples include student playing a game, sharing markers with a peer, helping a peer with a task, and making a statement in response to a question.

Solving Problems (SP): Student demonstrates overt physical or verbal behavior with the clear intent of solving or managing a confrontational or conflictual situation with another. This includes overt attempts to maintain self-control, use problem-solving steps (i.e., identify problem, consider alternatives and consequences, decide on best choice, and act out best choice), compromise, or negotiate with peer. Examples include student counting to five, offering to take turns to resolve conflict, making statements such as "Why don't we look at the directions?"

Negative Social Behaviors (S-)

Verbal Aggression (VA): Student makes a threatening, derogatory, or provocative statement or gesture toward another person. Examples include insults, threats, critical statements, inappropriate yelling, swearing, name calling, and physical gestures meant to convey a negative message.

Physical Aggression (PA): Student performs an overt, physical behavior that has the clear potential of inflicting physical harm or damage, or of provoking a confrontation. Examples include hitting, kicking, pushing, biting, tripping, throwing an object, and punching a wall.

Social Noncompliance (SN): Student makes an overt statement or nonaggressive action with the clear intent of breaking a known rule or evading an adult directive (when the behavior is aggressive, PA or VA is coded). Examples include refusing to answer a question posed to him/her, purposeful rule breaking in games, failing to wait for a turn, and failing to follow specified adult directions.

Isolated (IS): Student purposefully fails to interact or participate with others and engages in activity that is separate from peers and adults. Examples include coloring alone at table, writing on chalkboard by self, reading to self, wandering around room with no interaction, and watching ongoing activity with no attempt to interact.

consistent basis. For example, Bubba might be able to solve arguments with his peers in some classroom situations when his teacher is present; however, he might routinely become enraged on the playground and rather than resolve arguments calmly, allow them to escalate into full-fledged fights. If this is the case, you will want to work at increasing the frequency of occasions in which Bubba solves arguments calmly. Positive reinforcement in the form of praise, activities, or

Figure 2-7

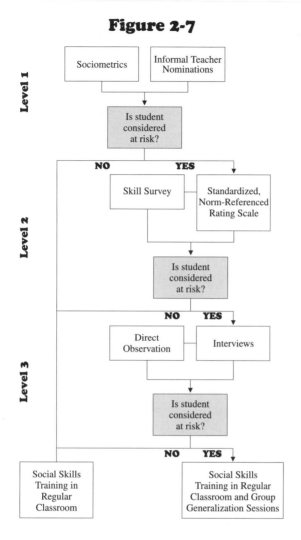

Examples of Social Skills

Social Entry Behaviors:
- Using body basics
- Starting a conversation
- Joining in
- Noticing feelings

Maintaining Interaction Behaviors:
- Keeping a conversation going
- Playing cooperatively
- Expressing feelings

Solving Problems:
- Solving problems
- Dealing with teasing
- Dealing with losing
- Dealing with being left out
- Using self-control
- Accepting "No"

concrete rewards, in conjunction with self-management strategies such as self-monitoring and goal setting, are often useful.

In reality, most social skills programs, including this one for Tough Kids, incorporate some procedures for skill deficits and some for performance deficits (modeling, coaching, cognitive strategies, self-management, and positive reinforcement). In this way, the most meaningful strategies that directly teach and promote the use of prosocial skills can be incorporated into treatment programs.

How To Box 2-5

Guidelines for Selecting Social Skills

1. Collect information from parents, teachers, and others who interact with the members of your group on a regular basis. Particularly useful information can be obtained using the *Skills Survey* (*SS*) (see Figure 2-3).

2. If a general social skills scale is used, you can score it as follows. First, following the instructions in the published manual, compute total scores to obtain an idea of the extent of concerns raised by respondents (parents, teachers, and students if possible). Then look at each item and list those that receive the lowest ratings. Highlight those items that are consistently rated low by several respondents.

3. On the *Skills Survey*, compile responses for each student individually, and summarize ratings for the group:

   - Generate individual profiles by computing item means for each student. In other words, sum the ratings that were provided by each respondent (teacher, parent, others) for each item and divide by the total number of respondents.

   - Generate a group profile by averaging students' item scores. In other words, compute a mean for each item by adding each student's average item score and dividing by the total number of students.

   - Make a list of the eight skills that receive the highest (most problematic) ratings in order to be addressed in ten-week small groups. (Remember that the first and last weeks are reserved for assessment and review.)

4. Conduct direct observations in the classroom, playground, and other school settings to verify problem areas and to document Tough Kids' social concerns.

Summary

A thorough multi-source, multi-method, and multi-setting assessment approach is necessary when considering a social skills training program. The purposes of assessment include identification of Tough Kids with social skills deficits (especially when small group social skills training will be conducted), selection of intervention targets, and evaluation of intervention outcomes.

A multi-gating assessment procedure was presented to help you select Tough Kids in need of social skills

training. Careful assessment will also allow you to identify specific social deficits of Tough Kids, as well as to determine whether their deficits are **skill deficits** (they do not know how to perform the skill) or **performance deficits** (they know how but simply do not perform the skill). A number of assessment methods should be combined to get a comprehensive picture of Tough Kids' social problems, including nominations and sociometrics (at Step 1), rating scales (at Step 2), and interviews and direct observations (at Step 3). The information you obtain from these assessments can be combined on an *Assessment Summary* like the one shown in Figure 2-8.

In the next chapter, a number of treatment methods will be presented. Also, a social skills program for Tough Kids that can be implemented in small groups, classrooms, or across the entire school is outlined. You will see that all of the most common treatment strategies are incorporated into the program. However, the treatment components that you will emphasize in your program (whether they be modeling and role play, or positive reinforcement and self-monitoring) should be based on the outcomes of your assessment; that is, on whether the Tough Kids demonstrate skill or performance deficits. In addition, a key component to social skills training must be on the generalization of social skills to the natural settings in which the Tough Kids interact with their peers. Specific procedures for encouraging Tough Kids to use their newly learned social skills in the "real world" are described in Chapter 4.

> **The purposes of assessment include identification of Tough Kids with social skills deficits. . . , selection of intervention targets, and evaluation of intervention outcomes."**

Figure 2-8

Assessment Summary

Student's Name: _____ Date: _____
Teacher's Name: _____ Grade: _____
Parent's Name: _____ Date of Birth: _____

	Pretest	Posttest
Nomination/ Ranking		
Sociometric Classification		
Rating Scale Scores General Scale Specific Scale		
Interviews Parent Teacher Student		
Observations		
Skills Needed to Teach		
Comments		

© 1995 by Sheridan, S.M. Available from Sopris West: Longmont, CO. (800) 547-6747
Part I—Social Skills Concepts

CHAPTER 2

Reproducibles

Tough Kid
Teacher Nomination

Teacher's Name: _____Grade:_____

A social skills treatment program will be offered for students in this school. The students who are expected to benefit most from the program are those who:

- Have few friends
- Frequently fight or argue with classmates
- Blame others for problems that arise
- Do not show an ability to solve problems with classmates
- Fail to use self-control
- Are not well liked by others

You know the students in your classroom better than anyone! So, I would appreciate it if you could take a few minutes to think about your class and list on the lines below no more than five students who have difficulties such as the ones listed above. Once I have received your nominations, I will follow up with you regarding the next step of assessment. Thank you!

1. _____
2. _____
3. _____
4. _____
5. _____

Student Sociometric

On the lines below, you will be asked to name some classmates. The reason you are being asked to do this is to learn more about children's friendships. Please do not put your name on this paper. Your answers will not be known by anyone. Please do not tell anyone how you answered, and do not talk about this activity with your classmates once you have finished. Thank you!

1. List the names of three classmates with whom you like to play:

   _____

   _____

   _____

2. List the names of three classmates with whom you do **not** like to play:

   _____

   _____

   _____

3. List the names of three classmates whom you would invite to your birthday party:

   _____

   _____

   _____

4. List the names of three classmates whom you would **not** invite to a birthday party:

   _____

   _____

   _____

© 1995 by Sheridan, S.M. Available from Sopris West: Longmont, CO. (800) 547-6747

Skills Survey

Student's Name: _____ Date: _____

Age:_____

The goal of the Social Skills Group is to identify specific areas in which students are experiencing difficulties, as well as to teach them positive social skills and behaviors in these problem areas. The behaviors listed below are several possible skill areas that may be targeted in the group. Your responses on this form will help us to identify areas that are problematic for students, and will assist in selecting specific skills to cover each week.

Using the scale of 1-4 listed below, please rate the degree to which each skill is a problem for the student. Thank you for your help.

1 - Never a problem
2 - Sometimes a problem
3 - Usually a problem
4 - Almost always a problem

Noticing and Talking About Feelings	1	2	3	4
Starting a Conversation	1	2	3	4
Joining In	1	2	3	4
Playing Cooperatively	1	2	3	4
Keeping a Conversation Going	1	2	3	4
Solving Problems	1	2	3	4
Solving Arguments	1	2	3	4
Dealing With Teasing	1	2	3	4
Dealing With Being Left Out	1	2	3	4
Using Self-Control	1	2	3	4
Accepting "No"	1	2	3	4

Part I—Social Skills Concepts

Social Skills Interview

Student's Name: _____ Date: _____

Teacher's Name: _____ Grade: _____

Parent's Name: _____ Date of Birth: _____

1. What are the specific concerns you have about _____'s social skills?

2. Which of these is the most problematic?

3. How often does it occur and how long has it been a problem?

4. Where does it occur?

5. What happens before the problem behavior?

6. What happens after the problem behavior?

7. What school or classroom procedures or rules are in place?

8. What do you expect of the student? What would be a reasonable goal for him/her?

9. What are some things the student excels at? What are his/her strengths? What does he/she like?

10. How and when can the problem be observed? How can data be collected on the problem?

Student Social Skills Interview

Student's Name: _____ Date: _____

Teacher's Name: _____ Grade: _____

Parent's Name: _____ Date of Birth: _____

1. Tell me about yourself. What do you like to do?

2. Tell me about your friends. How many do you have? Who is your best friend? What do you like to do with your friends?

3. What do you want to happen when you play with friends? What usually happens?

4. Everyone has problems once in a while with their friends. What kinds of problems do you have with your friends? Tell me about the last time you had a problem with a friend.

5. How do you usually solve your problems with friends? How did you solve the last problem you had with a friend?

6. Are there other ways that you could have solved the problem? (List the solutions provided by the student.)

   Solutions:
   6a._____
   6b._____
   6c._____
   6d._____
   6e._____

7. Looking at the list, what might happen if you did each of the things you just mentioned? (List the consequences provided by the student.)

   Consequences:
   7a._____
   7b._____
   7c._____
   7d._____
   7e._____

8. Are friends important? Why or why not?

9. If you could change one thing about yourself or your friendships, what would it be?

Part I—Social Skills Concepts

Social Skills Direct Observation

Student's Name: _____ Date: _____

Setting: _____ Grade: _____

		A (15 seconds)	B (30 seconds)	C (45 seconds)	D (60 seconds)
1	S+	SE PC SP	SE PC SP	SE PC SP	SE PC SP
	S-	VA PA SN IS	VA PA SN IS	VA PA SN IS	VA PA SN IS
2	S+	SE PC SP	SE PC SP	SE PC SP	SE PC SP
	S-	VA PA SN IS	VA PA SN IS	VA PA SN IS	VA PA SN IS
3	S+	SE PC SP	SE PC SP	SE PC SP	SE PC SP
	S-	VA PA SN IS	VA PA SN IS	VA PA SN IS	VA PA SN IS
4	S+	SE PC SP	SE PC SP	SE PC SP	SE PC SP
	S-	VA PA SN IS	VA PA SN IS	VA PA SN IS	VA PA SN IS
5	S+	SE PC SP	SE PC SP	SE PC SP	SE PC SP
	S-	VA PA SN IS	VA PA SN IS	VA PA SN IS	VA PA SN IS
6	S+	SE PC SP	SE PC SP	SE PC SP	SE PC SP
	S-	VA PA SN IS	VA PA SN IS	VA PA SN IS	VA PA SN IS
7	S+	SE PC SP	SE PC SP	SE PC SP	SE PC SP
	S-	VA PA SN IS	VA PA SN IS	VA PA SN IS	VA PA SN IS
8	S+	SE PC SP	SE PC SP	SE PC SP	SE PC SP
	S-	VA PA SN IS	VA PA SN IS	VA PA SN IS	VA PA SN IS
9	S+	SE PC SP	SE PC SP	SE PC SP	SE PC SP
	S-	VA PA SN IS	VA PA SN IS	VA PA SN IS	VA PA SN IS
10	S+	SE PC SP	SE PC SP	SE PC SP	SE PC SP
	S-	VA PA SN IS	VA PA SN IS	VA PA SN IS	VA PA SN IS
11	S+	SE PC SP	SE PC SP	SE PC SP	SE PC SP
	S-	VA PA SN IS	VA PA SN IS	VA PA SN IS	VA PA SN IS

Part I—Social Skills Concepts

Social Skills Direct Observation cont'd

		A (15 seconds)	B (30 seconds)	C (45 seconds)	D (60 seconds)
12	S+	SE PC SP	SE PC SP	SE PC SP	SE PC SP
	S-	VA PA SN IS	VA PA SN IS	VA PA SN IS	VA PA SN IS
13	S+	SE PC SP	SE PC SP	SE PC SP	SE PC SP
	S-	VA PA SN IS	VA PA SN IS	VA PA SN IS	VA PA SN IS
14	S+	SE PC SP	SE PC SP	SE PC SP	SE PC SP
	S-	VA PA SN IS	VA PA SN IS	VA PA SN IS	VA PA SN IS
15	S+	SE PC SP	SE PC SP	SE PC SP	SE PC SP
	S-	VA PA SN IS	VA PA SN IS	VA PA SN IS	VA PA SN IS
16	S+	SE PC SP	SE PC SP	SE PC SP	SE PC SP
	S-	VA PA SN IS	VA PA SN IS	VA PA SN IS	VA PA SN IS
17	S+	SE PC SP	SE PC SP	SE PC SP	SE PC SP
	S-	VA PA SN IS	VA PA SN IS	VA PA SN IS	VA PA SN IS
18	S+	SE PC SP	SE PC SP	SE PC SP	SE PC SP
	S-	VA PA SN IS	VA PA SN IS	VA PA SN IS	VA PA SN IS
19	S+	SE PC SP	SE PC SP	SE PC SP	SE PC SP
	S-	VA PA SN IS	VA PA SN IS	VA PA SN IS	VA PA SN IS
20	S+	SE PC SP	SE PC SP	SE PC SP	SE PC SP
	S-	VA PA SN IS	VA PA SN IS	VA PA SN IS	VA PA SN IS

Summary Table

Count the total number of slashes made for each behavior. Record the totals on the lines below. Divide the number of intervals observed and report the rate for each behavior.

		Total	#Intervals	Rate			Total	#Intervals	Rate
S+:	SE	____	/ ____	=	S-:	VA	____	/ ____	=
	PC	____	/ ____	=		PA	____	/ ____	=
	SP	____	/ ____	=		SN	____	/ ____	=
						IS	____	/ ____	=

Assessment Summary

Student's Name: _____ Date: _____

Teacher's Name: _____ Grade: _____

Parent's Name: _____ Date of Birth: _____

	Pretest	Posttest
Nomination/ Ranking		
Sociometric Classification		
Rating Scale Scores General Scale Specific Scale		
Interviews Parent Teacher Student		
Observations		
Skills Needed to Teach		
Comments		

Part I—Social Skills Concepts

Chapter 3

Three Levels of Social Skills Training

There are many ways to conduct social skills training. Because the skills that are being described are **social** (they have to do with interactions and relationships), the most effective and sensible way to intervene is in social **groups** (as compared to interventions that are delivered individually or apart from others). This allows Tough Kids immediate opportunities to practice the skills that are being taught, as well as receive immediate feedback from adult leaders and peers.

Once you decide that a social skills group is necessary, you will need to decide on the size and structure of the group. For example, you should determine whether only a small group of four to eight students will receive treatment, or if the needs of a classroom or a school warrant a more comprehensive approach. The basic procedures outlined in this book have been used in small groups of four to eight students (Sheridan, Dee, Morgan, McCormick, & Walker, 1996). They have also been used with classrooms of students. In some cases, entire schools set up a school-wide program to teach students basic skills and to encourage them to use these skills in everyday situations (Jones et. al., 1993). In this chapter, each of these models (small group, classroom, and school-wide programs) will be discussed to help you set up a social skills training procedure that is suited to your needs.

Small Group Social Skills Training

The most common method for conducting social skills training is through small groups. The Tough Kid assessment procedures lend themselves very nicely to working with small groups of students in 60-minute sessions.

There are several important points to consider when running a small group social skills intervention. These include the age and developmental level of students with whom you will be working, the size of the group, the number of boys and of girls, number and role of the leaders, and the amount of contact you will have with other persons in the students' lives (such as teachers and parents).

Age and Developmental Level

The social skills program for Tough Kids presented in this book was developed for and tested on students between the ages of 8 and 12. Similar procedures have been used with students as young as six, as well as with students into their teenage years. However, the activities used in groups (e.g., discussion, role play, homework, and feedback)

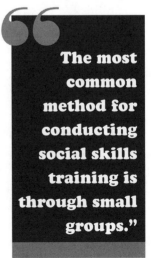

"The most common method for conducting social skills training is through small groups."

seem best suited for Tough Kids in the elementary school years (between third and sixth grade).

When setting up a small group, it is important to think about the similarity in age among potential members; it is usually a good idea to see that group members all fall within a two- to three-year age range or developmental level. This will make it easier to manage behaviors in the group, minimize boredom, and keep discussions focused and relevant. For example, think about a group comprised of four 12-year old and two eight-year old Tough Kids. Because the social issues and difficulties facing an eight-year old, third grade student are often quite different than those facing students entering middle school, such a group might be difficult to manage. The same basic social skills (such as having conversations or using self-control) will most likely apply; however, the examples, situations, and reinforcers used for students of different age and developmental levels may not.

A special note should be made about students with certain disabilities and their ability to benefit from the group procedures. In general, the format of the small group sessions requires cognitive and language abilities within the average range. This is true because of the rate at which information is presented, the thought processes required of students to consider choices and consequences of behaviors, and the need to imagine oneself in various social situations. Students with below average cognitive abilities (e.g., students with learning disabilities) or very deficient processing capabilities (e.g., students with severe communication disorders), often have a difficult time in social skills assessment groups.

Size of Group

The number of students to include in your small group is another important decision to make prior to beginning assessment. In general, groups with fewer than four or more than eight students are not recommended. One of the benefits of involving Tough Kids in groups is that the group will give them opportunities to practice new skills with other students; ideally, with five or six other

students. Groups that are too small do not provide the necessary variety of peers with whom Tough Kids must learn to get along. Small groups are in jeopardy if one or more members misses a session or drops out. On the other hand, groups of more than eight students often become difficult to manage. With large groups, there is usually not enough time to allow all students to partake in discussions, role plays, and feedback. Also, Tough Kids might become distracted, bored, or oppositional if they are not kept busy and engaged during group time. In addition, an even number of students is usually desirable (it allows easy pairing in role plays), but this is not required. Ideally, a small group of five, six, or seven students, with one or two leaders, seems to be the most effective size.

Number of Boys and of Girls

Both boys and girls can have problems with friends. There is no reason why boys and girls should not be included in the same group. It is generally important, however, not to have only one female in a group of males or vice versa; at least two or three females and two or three males is appropriate.

There are important social skills that boys and girls can learn from each other. For example, when involved together in social skills training, they can begin to develop an understanding of what is important to each other. Boys and girls can also learn about each other's thoughts and feelings in various situations, and about appropriate ways to provide feedback to each other.

Consider Bubba, for example. He is usually not asked by other students to play at recess. When he tries to join into a game, he does so by cutting into line, yelling, or using other bullying tactics. When these do not work (and they usually do not), he huffs away angrily. Other days you might see him watch from the sidelines while the other boys play a game such as four square or catch. When he gets bored, he wanders over to the section where girls are jumping rope and begins harassing them by trying to interfere or take away their ropes. He thinks this is fun. Unfortunately, his female peers begin to think of him as a bully and a nuisance and will actively avoid and reject him in all sorts of situations inside and outside of the school building. By including both girls and boys in a group, all students might learn how to get along better and provide helpful feedback to each other. Bubba might also begin to learn how others perceive his "playful" (irritating!) behavior. In general, inappropriate behaviors of all students, such as fighting, tattling, and talking back can be dealt with directly in social skills groups.

Recruiting Students Into Small Groups

Once you have decided to conduct a small group, you will need to do some "shopping" for students to be involved. In most cases, this will not be a difficult task. In fact, you may have more students identified as in need of social skills training than you are able to include. (This might actually be a "red flag" that a more comprehensive approach, such as classroom-based or school-wide training, is necessary.)

There are several considerations to keep in mind when recruiting and selecting students to be part of the group. In general, it is important to identify a group of students who have some problems or concerns in common. For example, the students in your group might have particular difficulty using self-control and solving problems. Similarities like these will make it easier for you to deal with specific issues that each student can relate to. Adding an extremely withdrawn or shy student into a group of impulsive or aggressive students would not be a good match between the shy student's needs and the emphasis of the group. Keep in mind, though, that a group comprised of all really Tough Kids may not be a good idea either. It is recommended that you balance the group with some students whose problems are less severe, but still on the same general continuum.

In addition to the already recommended recruitment techniques—the importance of having all

students within a year or two of each other, and of making sure that there is more than only one girl or only one boy in the group—other steps for recruiting students are presented in How To Box 3-1.

"Am I in the right place?"

Number of Leaders

Two leaders are generally necessary to conduct an effective social skills group. It is not impossible to lead a group alone, but in a good group, there are several activities to keep track of and behaviors to manage. (Remember, we are working with Tough Kids!) Because of this, groups that are conducted by co-leaders tend to have an advantage. The roles and responsibilities of co-leaders should be very clear in order to avoid confusion about how to conduct the group. It is often useful to assign one leader the task of leading the group (leading discussions, role plays, and making sure the group members understand important points). The other leader can then be responsible for watching for behavior problems and helping students pay attention. This co-leader can effectively "float" around the group providing individualized feedback (e.g., praise and corrective feedback) and prompting students to use certain skills. The second leader can also help model appropriate

> **Groups that are conducted by co-leaders tend to have an advantage."**

How To Box 3-1

Recruiting Students for Small Group Social Skills Training

1. "Advertise" your interest in conducting a small group. This can be done by talking to teachers and parents of students who might be appropriate for the group, or by placing announcements in teachers' mailboxes.

2. Describe the type of student who would be appropriate for your social skills group. For example, let teachers and parents know if you intend to work with all boys, all girls, or a combination. Describe the types of behavioral and social problems that will be addressed in the group. For example, you might deal primarily with students who have outward behavior and social problems such as fighting, arguing, and bullying.

3. Ask teachers for nominations of students in their classroom who meet the general criteria for your group. You might use a form

such as the *Tough Kid Teacher Nomination* presented in Figure 2-1 (Chapter 2).

4. Using procedures (skills surveys, interviews, and direct observations) described in Chapter 2, conduct a more thorough assessment of the students who were referred. This will help you narrow down the group into a manageable number. When more students are nominated than you can manage in one group, try to identify your participants by: (a) severity of need, and (b) similarity of social problems. Consider conducting more than one group, or classroom-based groups if there are several students nominated.

5. Obtain formal parental consent before including any student in small group social skills training.

---

social skills and set up and supervise role plays as necessary.

Role of Parents and Teachers

Another point to think about when planning social skills groups is the amount of contact and participation you can expect from other adults in the Tough Kids' lives. For example, depending on where you conduct the social skills training, you may or may not have ongoing contact with teachers or parents. For example, if you meet at a school, you will have a lot of chances to speak with teachers, recess monitors, and hopefully, parents of Tough Kids. It is very important to try to recruit them to help teach students social skills from the start and to communicate with them often throughout the duration of the group. Such involvement is especially important to help Tough Kids generalize their newly learned social skills

to the "real world." (More will be discussed on the topic of generalization in Chapter 4.)

There are many ways to encourage parent involvement in social skills training. A related book ("Social Skills for the Tough Kid: A Program for Parents" by S. Sheridan and C. Dee) is available that helps school psychologists, counselors, social workers, or others set up and conduct a training program for parents to continue working on social skills with Tough Kids at home. It is strongly recommended that you look at this program and consider running groups for parents at the same time you run groups for Tough Kids. If it is not feasible to run such a program, there are components of it that can be used to communicate with parents about the social skills program. For example, two or three parent sessions (rather than an entire ten-week program) can be conducted to share materials, ideas, and observations. (Make sure they are scheduled at a time when parents can attend, such as after school or in the evening.) A Home-School Note program or contract system can be used where Tough Kids receive social skills points from teachers or group leaders, which are cashed in for reinforcers or consequences that are delivered at home. An example of a useful social skills *Home-School Note* is presented in Figure 3-1.

Teachers of students in the social skills groups should also be involved in the program as much as possible. In the next sections, class- and school-wide applications of social skills training are discussed. Obviously, classroom teachers need to be highly involved when such programs are conducted in the classroom. But when small group interventions are used (students are taken out of the classroom), teachers' roles tend to be less clear. At a minimum, group leaders should frequently consult and communicate with the teachers. There are many important topics to discuss with teachers, including the skills being

taught, the steps necessary for Tough Kids to demonstrate the skills appropriately, procedures that they can use to prompt Tough Kids to use social skills in the classroom, and general information about their students' performances in the group. It is also essential that group leaders ask teachers for information, such as the teachers' specific concerns with students (see Chapter 2 for a discussion of teacher referrals and interviews), and their observations of any behavioral changes once the group is underway.

A communication system using a standard feedback form, such as the one in Figure 3-2, can be very helpful in involving parents and teachers. On this form (the *Weekly Social Skills Record*), group leaders provide teachers and parents with information on the skill being taught (including the steps), personal goals being worked on for each student, and any other pertinent information about students' behaviors and performances in the group. Teachers and parents, in return, can provide information about how often and how effectively students are using their new skills. A simple rating scale is provided on the *Weekly*

Figure 3-1

Home-School Note

Name: _____   Date: _____

Stars will be given for using your social skills every day. If _____ stars are earned each day, you earn _____!

	MON	TUE	WED	THUR	FRI
Joined In/ Started Conversations					
Played Cooperatively					
Solved Problems Calmly					
Used Self-Control					
TOTAL					
Initials					

Rating Scale: Used the skill a lot! = 2 points
Used the skill one or two times = 1 point
Did not use the skill = 0 points

© 1995 by Sheridan, S.M. Available from Sopris West: Longmont, CO. (800) 547-6747
Part I—Social Skills Concepts

Figure 3-2

Weekly Social Skills Record

Student's Name: _____ Week of: _____

Student's Personal Goal for the Week: _____
_____

This Week's Social Skill: _____

Steps: 1.
2.
3.
4.
5.

1. Did you see the student use this skill during the week?   ☐ Yes   ☐ No
    If yes, approximately how many times?   ☐ 1-2   ☐ 3-4   ☐ 5-6   ☐ 7+
    If no, were there opportunities when the student could have used the skill?
    ☐ Yes   ☐ No

2. Place a check by any other skills you observed the student using during the week.
    ___ _____
    ___ _____
    ___ _____
    ___ _____
    ___ _____

3. Rate the student's general social interactions with his/her peers during the week:
    ☐ Improving
    ☐ Staying about the same
    ☐ Getting worse

4. Rate the student's overall social interactions:
    ☐ Improving
    ☐ Staying about the same
    ☐ Getting worse

© 1995 by Sheridan, S.M. Available from Sopris West: Longmont, CO. (800) 547-6747
Part I—Social Skills Concepts

Social Skills Record to provide such feedback. Be sure to also ask for other comments and concerns to allow them to elaborate if necessary.

Classroom-Based Social Skills Training

When was the last time you heard (or used) the phrase "That fifth (or third, or sixth) grade! I do not know what it is about them, but they're a really Tough Bunch this year!" Such a statement should suggest a larger social skills group intervention, such as one geared toward an entire classroom. The procedures described in this book lend themselves well to classroom programs; however, there are some things to consider before jumping in at this level. These considerations include the grade level of students, length of classroom training sessions, availability of leaders, methods of tracking students' participation and performance, and the desirability of group-based reinforcement programs.

Grade Level of Students

In an earlier section on small group training procedures, it was suggested that the Tough Kid social skills program is most appropriate for students between the ages of 8 and 12. This generally translates into classrooms covering grades third through seventh. The procedures in this program require an ability to role play and think about social situations in terms of choices and consequences. There are also many written materials such as skill charts, homework sheets, and cue cards. The procedures presented here are likely to be too advanced for students younger than third grade.

> " ... think about the social skills curriculum as a normal part of the school week, much like social studies or geography."

Frequency and Length of Classroom Training Sessions

In small group social skills training, the sessions are conducted once per week and usually last 60 minutes. The weekly session format is important because it allows for frequent meetings, but also for time to practice between sessions. In classroom-based social skills programs, weekly sessions are strongly recommended for the same reasons. Plus, when they are scheduled at the same time each week, it encourages both the teachers and students to think about the social skills curriculum as a normal part of the school week, much like social studies or geography. It also helps teachers in planning their weekly activities and lesson plans because they can write in "social skills" as an event that occurs on the same day and at the same time each week.

Although weekly sessions are important in classroom-based programs, it is possible that 60-minute sessions may not always seem feasible. This may be true whether you are a classroom teacher "giving up" time otherwise devoted to teaching academics, or whether you are a counselor or school psychologist helping to run classroom groups in more than one grade.

Before resigning to the fact that these procedures take too much time, consider how much more pleasant your life would be if all of the students for whom you were responsible used good manners, solved problems peacefully, and played together in a positive manner. Think of how effectively you might use the time you once spent reprimanding and correcting students. In the long run, social skills programs might give you **more** time (rather than less) to devote to using your creative talents, teaching important academic skills, or preventing future problems from occurring. If it still seems impossible to spend 60 minutes on social skills each week, it is recommended that you devote most of the time to practice (modeling and role play) and to setting up behavioral programs for generalization purposes, and less time in group discussions.

Availability of Leaders

Perhaps one of the biggest considerations in deciding whether to try a classroom-based social skills group concerns the question of "Who will run the sessions?" Teachers may feel ill prepared to attempt such an undertaking since few classroom teachers have had any formal training in social skills. Support staff, such as school psychologists, school counselors, or social workers, seem to be likely candidates to conduct classroom-based programs, but it is likely they will not have firsthand knowledge and experience with the group of students in question. They also carry notoriously high caseloads with demands placed on them by administrators, parents, etc., and would have to balance classroom social skills training with other school responsibilities.

The best approach to running social skills programs in the classroom is one in which a teacher works closely with a support person. It is essential that teachers and support staff work collaboratively and share their own unique perspectives and talents to make the program a success. Together, these individuals can identify the skills to be taught, outline the specific procedures they will use for social skills training, and decide on how to evaluate student performance. Teachers are important in developing and implementing the program because they are the experts when it comes to their classroom and the students in it. Certified support staff are important because they can provide an "objective eye," and may have special training or experience running social skills groups. In this sense, they can help teachers learn how to conduct social skills lessons.

There are many advantages to having two leaders in classroom-based social skills programs. From a practical standpoint, a social skills training program can easily become too big to manage alone, especially given all of the other things that have to be done on a daily basis! In the classroom training sessions, the co-leaders can take turns leading the group, while the second person watches for behavior problems or inattentiveness. Two leaders are also useful for demonstrating a particular skill, modeling good social skills, and observing students' role plays. For example, students in the class can be split up into two groups (with one leader assigned to each), or into smaller groups wherein each leader can circulate and observe a portion of the role play. Either of these formats provides more opportunities for each student to role play the target skill, and it is easier to monitor students with two leaders.

> **Teachers are important in developing and implementing the program because they are the experts when it comes to their classroom and the students in it.**

When pairing students up for small group role plays, be careful of your selections. For example, if you know that Bubba has problems with a particular student in the class, do not start the training with the two of them as partners. After a few weeks you might want to try having them work together, but only after they each show that they are able to use appropriate self-control in tenuous situations.

Ideally, after co-conducting several social skills lessons in the classroom, the teacher will feel comfortable in this new role. At this point, it might be useful for the certified support person (e.g., the school counselor or social worker) to fade his/her involvement and introduce a volunteer into the program to help the teacher complete the lessons. Individuals such as parents, office staff, and recess aides might be very helpful in this role. Parents or other volunteers are especially useful in programs that are scheduled to continue throughout the school year. This also allows the support staff to circulate to other teachers and classrooms to help set up additional classroom-based social skills programs.

Figure 3-3

Self-Assessment for Group Sessions

Student's Name: _____ Date: _____

Social Skill of the Day: _____

How well did I:

	Not very well	OK	Great
• Pay attention?	1	2	3
• Discuss the topic and give examples?	1	2	3
• Think of personal examples?	1	2	3
• Practice role playing the skill?	1	2	3
• Work on my personal goal?	1	2	3
• Give others feedback?	1	2	3
• Set goals and complete a contract?	1	2	3

Student's Signature: _____

Leader's Signature: _____

© 1995 by Sheridan, S.M. Available from Sopris West: Longmont, CO. (800) 547-6747
Part I—Social Skills Concepts

Monitoring Participation and Performance

One possible difficulty with classroom-based programs is that you may not be able to carefully monitor how students, including Tough Kids, are learning and using the new skills in various environments. Simple, easy-to-use monitoring procedures should be used to maintain a rough gauge of their performances. Whenever possible, self-monitoring procedures should be built into the social skills program to make sure that some record is being kept.

Self-monitoring is an easy, cost-efficient way to keep track of how a student is doing both in the social skills training session and between sessions in natural social situations. It involves having the Tough Kids keep a record of their own behaviors. In the training session students can keep track of behaviors, such as how many times they volunteer to answer a question, relate personal examples of situations in which they could

practice the weekly skill, and how they do in role play. They can also rate themselves on how they think they performed during a social skills class on a three- or five-point scale, such as the one in Figure 3-3.

Outside of the social skills training session, students should be expected to self-monitor their use of the social skills being taught. A simple chart system is useful because it is straightforward and easy. A chart such as the one in Figure 3-4 can be used by asking students to simply mark, with a check, sticker, star, etc., each time they use the skill being taught under the appropriate day of the week. Some students are able to record these events easily; others need more instruction to make sure they know what to do. Other strategies to increase the usefulness of self-monitoring are listed in How To Box 3-2.

Reinforcement Systems

Keeping an entire class of students motivated and interested in the social skills lessons from week to week can be one of the biggest challenges in classroom-based programs. Yet, there are several ways that incentives can be built into the program to maximize the continued involvement of all students. Many positive reinforcement procedures are discussed in Chapter 4, including praise, weekly tangible reinforcers (e.g., Mystery Motivators, Spinners, and Homework Charts) and a group party. These can all be

Figure 3-4

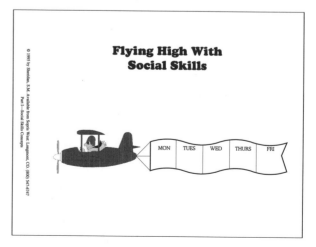

How To Box 3-2

Strategies to Increase the Usefulness of Self-Monitoring

Tough Kids will not necessarily know how to be good observers and recorders of their own behaviors, yet these are precisely the skills that are necessary in order to be good at self-monitoring. When implementing a self-monitoring system, consider the following suggestions:

1. *Teach students how to self-monitor.* Show them the chart that will be used and tell them an effective rationale for why it is important. Show them how to keep track of their behaviors on a chart using tally marks, stickers, stars, smiley faces, or whatever else they are interested in using.

2. *Make sure students know what behaviors they are self-monitoring.* Define the behaviors clearly for the Tough Kids, rather than expecting that they will know what you mean. For example, your idea of "using an appropriate voice" or "solving problems calmly" may be very different than theirs! Come to an agreement on what the behavior and definition means, and demonstrate it if necessary.

3. *Keep the system simple.* The self-monitoring form should be fairly simple and straightforward. The procedures for tracking the behavior should be easy. For example, it is easier to place one simple mark on a chart at the end of recess or after a lesson than it is to bring forms onto the playground or interrupt activities to mark the sheet.

4. *Expect students to self-monitor only one or two behaviors at a time.* It is very important not to overwhelm students with too many behaviors to track at once. In general, Tough Kids can be expected to keep track of one or two behaviors, but probably not more than that.

5. *Have students practice self-monitoring before starting the program.* For example, they might practice with you during a role play situation the types of behaviors that would get marked and those that would not. Also, give them one or two days to get used to the system, to ask questions, and to receive feedback before beginning.

6. *Do periodic checks on the accuracy of self-monitoring.* Every once in a while (once or twice a week), keep your own record of how the student is behaving. Keep track of the same behaviors on a form similar to the one the Tough Kids are using. Let Tough Kids know that you will do this, but do not tell them when. When completed, compare your marks with the Tough Kids' and see how closely they match up. Consider linking accurate self-monitoring (e.g., 80% agreement between you and each student) with some type of reward, such as an extra five minutes of recess.

useful in classroom-based programs. When conducting social skills training for entire classes, group reinforcers are also important because of the added support and encouragement that students will likely provide each other when they have something at stake.

Classroom-based reinforcement systems require all students (or a large percentage of them) in a classroom to meet some basic criteria before the entire group earns a reward. For example, one method of a classroom-based reinforcement program requires the entire class to show an ability to use the weekly skill both inside and outside of the classroom. Each student could be required to perform a "perfect" role play in the classroom-based training session by following without instruction each of the steps involved in the social skill. Beyond that, they could earn a special ticket (see Figure 3-5) from recess monitors, office staff, or lunchroom aides when they use the skill outside of the classroom without being prompted. If all students in the class earn the ticket, the entire class could earn a party or other special event at the end of the week.

Another way to incorporate a motivator could be to break the class down into groups consisting of four students each. Social skills tickets could be earned when students demonstrate the weekly skill outside of the training session, but within the smaller groups. In addition a public posting system (see Figure 3-6) could be used in the classroom to keep track of the tickets earned by members of each group. The group earning the most tickets each week could receive special rewards.

School-Wide Social Skills Training

The social skills training program described in this book has been used successfully in a school-wide application. The procedures are discussed in an article by Jones, Sheridan, and Binns (1993).

There are many important considerations when trying to develop a school-wide social skills training program. It is especially important to give time and thought to procedures that might make the program work in your school. A first step is to look into things like the commitment of the school body to support the program, including the people available to help keep it alive. Preparation of key individuals—teachers, parents, and additional staff—is essential to running the program effectively. Also, it is necessary to identify the most reasonable way to put the pieces together into a meaningful program that is just the right fit for your school.

Figure 3-5

Figure 3-6

Part I—Social Skills Concepts

School Commitment

In a successful school-wide social skills program, administrators, teachers, staff, and others share commitment and ownership in the program. In an ideal situation, the entire school body (including the school principal, parents, support persons such as counselors and school psychologists, teachers, and students) will value the program and pay more than lip service to making it a success. For long-term success, the program must be an ongoing aspect of the school's activities, and not simply a project that only a few staff members are committed to.

"They'll never find me here."

Among the main individuals to support a school-wide social skills program, the **school administrator** is someone who can make or break a project's success at any stage of its existence. He/she can help set the standard (or tone) for the rest of the school if he/she is particularly in favor of the social skills program. He/she can provide financial assistance and staff release time to develop products, or purchase reinforcers or supplies. He/she can also make sure that incentives are offered to staff, parents, and students for their participation in the program. The school administrator

can schedule necessary activities, such as staff training and classroom sessions, to make sure that time is devoted to social skills training.

Teachers can demonstrate commitment to a school-wide social skills effort in a number of ways. They can help identify the needs of the school and their students and be an important part of selecting specific skills to be taught. They can make social skills part of their everyday classroom through activities such as conducting or co-conducting social skills training sessions, establishing a "social skills station" in their classroom where social skills homework can be turned in, and delivering praise and/or tickets to students who demonstrate appropriate social skills outside of the formal social skills instruction time. They can also provide grades on report cards for students' participation in the social skills curriculum. Importantly, they can set the stage for a healthy social skills environment by modeling behaviors that are expected of students, and by communicating to students (both directly and indirectly) that good social skills are as important as other academic skills like math, reading, and science.

Support staff, such as school psychologists, school counselors, social workers, nurses, and special education consultants, also play an essential role in the success of school-wide programs. First, it is likely that the school psychologist or social worker may be perceived as the "social skills expert" in the school building. In fact, it may be one of these individuals who initially identifies the need and develops procedures for a school-wide project. But it is also important that certified staff help promote the program in a practical way. This might take the form of helping conduct social skills training sessions in classrooms, delivering praise or points to students in the hallways or other school settings when they see the use of good social skills, or helping to evaluate the effects of the school-wide program.

There are also important roles for additional **school staff**, such as office help, custodians, lunch aides, bus drivers, and recess monitors. In

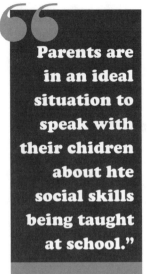

> **Parents are in an ideal situation to speak with their chidren about hte social skills being taught at school."**

fact, these individuals typically see students in "real" social situations when there may be little structure and great potential for mayhem. Support staff are quite helpful in providing immediate suggestions to students to use the skills they are learning in **actual social situations**, as well as reinforcing students for using appropriate social skills. They are also extremely important in helping students realize that it is appropriate and relevant to use their newly acquired social skills in actual play settings. For example, Bubba might be angry during recess when another student accidentally bumps into him. He has several choices at this point. He could: (1) calmly tell the student that he understands that accidents happen; (2) scream at the student and call him a clumsy oaf; or (3) beat the living daylights out of him!

"Is this the storm before the calm?"

In our experiences with Tough Kids, choice 1 rarely happens, but if it did, the lunchroom aide could provide lots of verbal reinforcement for dealing with the problem peacefully and successfully. Unfortunately, choices 2 and 3 seem most common; in these situations, the lunchroom aide could easily step in and prompt Bubba to use his problem-solving skills (it is likely that he will not even realize that they could apply

here). If he is able to solve the problem, he could receive reinforcement. If he still has difficulties, the aide could help him by modeling what it is he should do (the steps of problem solving) and asking him to use the steps in that situation.

An important group of persons that cannot be forgotten is **parents**. Parents are in an ideal situation to speak with their children about the social skills being taught at school, how they can be used on the playground and at home, and problems they may be having with their peers or classmates. If possible, they are often helpful in setting up Home-School Note programs (see Figure 3-1) that enable students' school behaviors, such as the use of social skills, to be reinforced at home. Parents might also be willing to volunteer to come into the school and help teach a social skills lesson in their child's classroom, or monitor social skills on the playground.

Preparation of Staff and Other Key Individuals

Once the key persons who will be involved in the school-wide social skills program are identified, it is important that some time and energy be spent preparing them for their role. If possible, at least two training sessions at the beginning of the school year and some "booster sessions" every few months are useful. How To Box 3-3 outlines the types of activities that are useful in staff training sessions. In general, one initial session can cover many important introductory topics, such as why it is important to do school-wide social skills training. Follow-up sessions can provide **skill building activities**, such as modeling and role play. Modeling is a useful strategy to demonstrate the behaviors and activities that you want others to use. For example, as a social skills leader, you might model for a custodian how to verbally reinforce a student when he is observed solving an argument calmly. Role play is a technique that allows persons to practice appropriate techniques and receive immediate feedback. For example, the custodian could be required to practice giving positive reinforcement to make sure that he can use it effectively.

How To Box 3-3

Outline of Activities to Include in Staff Training Sessions

Staff Training Session I

1. **Program Background and Rationale—** Discuss with the staff why a school-wide social skills program is necessary. Outline things such as the goals and objectives of the program, the skills that will be taught, and the importance of working together for success.

2. **Program Procedures**—Describe all of the components of the social skills training program. This discussion should be very specific, while still allowing time for questions from staff. Topics that should be included are:

   - How social skills for training will be selected.
   - The classroom-based social skills training sessions (including who will be responsible for leading the sessions and who will assist, an overview of the format, homework, and contracts).
   - The reinforcement system to be used (e.g., a token system with a school store or raffle, classroom-based programs, or individual contracts).
   - The importance of generalization strategies (reinforcing, prompting, and modeling skill use).

3. **Program Timeline and Other Logistical Issues**—Some attention should be paid to practical issues such as when the program will begin, how long it will last, who is responsible for coordinating the program, and who can answer questions.

4. **Setting Realistic Expectations**—It is very important for staff to realize that a school-wide social skills program is not always easy, and that changes in Tough Kids'

behaviors will not be immediate. Help them understand that some challenging situations are expected, and that some students may not cooperate all the time. Help them see that although the program will take time and effort on their part, the skills that are taught to students may translate into a more pleasant and effective classroom and school in the long run.

Staff Training Session II

1. **Social Skills Program Components—** Provide a quick review of what the school-wide social skills program will consist of.

2. **Social Skills Training Components—** Spend time outlining the activities of social skills training as they will occur in the classrooms. Give staff a detailed review of each step of training (include a discussion of the weekly review, introduction of a new skill, presentation of skill steps, modeling, role playing, and feedback). A good reference is Box 4-1, (Chapter 4). Ask for volunteers that might be available to help teachers conduct social skills training in the classrooms. These volunteers might include office staff, Chapter One teachers, custodians, bus drivers, or lunchroom aides.

3. **Illustrate Social Skills Training**—Go through each step involved in the social skills training and demonstrate what that part of the training session entails. Ask for volunteers to serve as students to make the illustration more realistic and meaningful.

(continued)

How To Box 3-3 cont'd

If available, videotapes of actual group sessions might be used for demonstration purposes.

4. **Role Play Social Skills Training Components**—Have staff break up into small groups, and practice each of the main components of social skills training. For example, they might practice reviewing the steps of solving problems, or modeling the skill of dealing with teasing. Give staff specific feedback on what they are doing well, and what they might try differently.

5. **Demonstrate and Practice Generalization Strategies**—Show staff Figure 4-9 (Chapter 4), which illustrates the use of reinforcement, prompting, and modeling to encourage students to use social skills outside of the training session. It is also useful to illustrate how the staff might use these strategies in everyday classroom and school situations (such as when passing out papers, helping students in the office, or monitoring students during recess).

6. **Ask for Additional Questions and Provide a Contact**—Encourage staff to ask questions during and after the training session; their questions will likely benefit everyone. Before ending the staff meeting, reassure staff that someone is always available to answer questions as they implement the school-wide social skills training program. Let them know how to get in touch with that person, and remind them that the whole school "is in this together!"

Booster sessions, conducted every two to three months throughout the duration of the program, are also helpful as a time for staff to regroup and review the social skills program. They provide an opportunity for program developers, social skills leaders, school staff, and parents to meet and compare their opinions on how the program is working. An informal format is recommended for booster sessions so that everyone can feel relaxed and encouraged to speak honestly about how things are going. Booster sessions should not, however, take the place of checking in frequently to ask about the program and what works or does not work in its day-to-day operation.

Putting the Pieces Together

There are several additional touches that can be used to make your school-wide program successful. First, it is useful to teach a school-wide **skill of the week** in order that all of the students and school staff are working on the same social skills at the same time. These skills should be prioritized by the school staff, using techniques described in Chapter 2. Second, to the greatest extent possible, several visual reminders of the weekly social skill (e.g., posters in the main school corridor, signs on the lunchroom walls, and notes home to parents) should be used. Verbal reminders are also helpful; these can take place in classrooms, on the playground, or even with announcements by the principal or another student over the school loudspeaker system. Students must be reminded over and over that social skills are a central part of their school experience.

Another component that might increase the success of a school-wide program is the use of a school-wide reinforcement program such as a lottery or store. For example, depending on what resources—money and materials—are available for the program, students might be able to earn tickets to be cashed in for prizes at a school store. Or, they might enter the tickets into a weekly (or daily) school lottery in which they can win lunch with the principal or a free hour within their school day. Ideas for setting up school-wide reinforcement programs are presented in How To Box 3-4.

Combining Approaches

In many cases, the extent of the social problems in a classroom or school may warrant the combination of large group (classroom- or school-based) and small group training approaches. This is particularly useful in situations where you identify a number of students with extensive social skills deficits, who may not receive enough attention in classroom training sessions. If a combined approach is possible, it is strongly recommended since it provides the toughest Tough Kids with a double dose of social skills training.

When using a combined large and small group approach, first use the multi-gating procedures described in Chapter 2 to identify those students who are in greatest need for intensive (small group) social skills training. Then arrange with classroom teachers a time (following their weekly classroom-based sessions) when you can work with a small group of students. The focus of small group sessions in this case should be **generalization** of skills they were taught in the

---

How To Box 3-4

Procedures for Setting Up School-Wide Reinforcement Programs

1. Work with the school administrator to obtain approval for establishing a school-wide reinforcement program. Inform him/her of the reasons such a program is necessary, and what benefits can be expected.

2. Pending the principal's support, solicit support and assistance from as many other members of the school staff (including volunteers) as possible. The administrator can be asked to make financial resources available. Others, such as the Parent-Teacher Association (PTA), paraprofessionals, and volunteers, might be requested to set up and run a school store or raffle.

3. If financial support is not available within the school, request support and donations from local businesses. For example, a local sports shop or department store might donate small items that can serve as reinforcers. Larger businesses might donate money to help produce tickets and other necessary supplies.

4. "Price" items in the store according to your perception of the students' interests in the items. For example, a small pencil eraser

might cost one ticket, whereas a can of soda might cost ten tickets. Include some less tangible items in the store, such as five extra minutes of recess, or the privilege of making a daily announcement on the school's loudspeaker system.

5. Instruct all school staff of the procedures for delivering tickets. Make sure they understand how students can earn the tickets and how and when they can be cashed in.

6. Describe the basics of the reinforcement program to students. Be sure that students understand:

   - How tickets are earned
   - How to save and spend tickets
   - Where the store is located and how it runs

7. With some Tough Kids, a penalty system might be included in the program. This system would require students to give up a certain amount of tickets that they have earned for engaging in very inappropriate, aggressive, or otherwise problematic behavior.

---

classroom session. The sessions should occur in settings where they will be expected to use the skill (e.g., on the playground or in the gymnasium). The activities in these small groups should include a review of the skill that was taught in the larger group and a brief discussion of its use to make sure that the students know the skill steps and how they are performed. Some modeling and role playing may be necessary if students are not clear about how to use the skill.

Students should then be allowed to engage in a small group activity that requires the skill. For example, they might play a board game to practice the skill of playing cooperatively. Leaders in these groups should be attentive to the students' appropriate and inappropriate (or lack of) use of social skills, and follow the generalization flowchart to provide feedback and reinforcement.

Summary

Three levels of social skills training were described in this chapter. First, small groups of four to eight students are commonly conducted. These groups can focus on specific skill deficits of students, but some deliberate efforts should be made to encourage students to use their newly learned behaviors in different settings. In general, the more the training setting is like that of the natural social settings within which the Tough Kids interact, the better. Also, it is useful to involve peers in training, as well as adults who can help students generalize their skills to new settings and situations.

The second level of social skills training is the classroom level. At this level, entire classrooms are involved in learning appropriate social skills. Teachers should be involved in classroom-based social skills training in as many ways as possible. For example, they can provide invaluable assessment information, help run group discussions, assist in modeling and role playing exercises, and help develop behavioral contracts. Classroom reinforcement programs are often useful to promote skill acquisition and use.

The third level of social skills training is the school-wide level. These social skills programs are valuable from both prevention and intervention standpoints. In this approach, the entire school body takes part in social skills training. All students and school staff work together to promote the use of good social skills. The program should be a central aspect of the school's mission, and staff training is necessary to ensure that all staff are able to assist in carrying out the objectives.

Finally, a combination of a large group (such as classroom- or school-wide) approach with a small group training component can be useful in addressing Tough Kids' social problems. By combining approaches, Tough Kids receive both group-based intervention in the context of the classroom, and individualized attention provided in the intensive small-group intervention.

CHAPTER 3

Reproducibles

Home-School Note

Name: _____ Date: _____

Stars will be given for using your social skills every day. If _____ stars are earned each day, you earn _____!

	MON	TUE	WED	THUR	FRI
Joined In/ Started Conversations					
Played Cooperatively					
Solved Problems Calmly					
Used Self-Control					
TOTAL					
Initials					

Rating Scale: Used the skill a lot! = 2 points
Used the skill one or two times = 1 point
Did not use the skill = 0 points

Weekly Social Skills Record

Student's Name: _____ Week of: _____

Student's Personal Goal for the Week: _____

_____

This Week's Social Skill: _____

Steps: 1.

         2.

         3.

         4.

         5.

1. Did you see the student use this skill during the week? ☐ Yes ☐ No

    If yes, approximately how many times? ☐ 1-2 ☐ 3-4 ☐ 5-6 ☐ 7+

    If no, were there opportunities when the student could have used the skill?

                                               ☐ Yes ☐ No

2. Place a check by any other skills you observed the student using during the week.

    ____ _____

    ____ _____

    ____ _____

    ____ _____

    ____ _____

    ____ _____

3. Rate the student's general social interactions with his/her peers during the week:

    ☐ Improving
    ☐ Staying about the same
    ☐ Getting worse

4. Rate the student's overall social interactions:

    ☐ Improving
    ☐ Staying about the same
    ☐ Getting worse

Self-Assessment for Group Sessions

Student's Name: _____ Date: _____

Social Skill of the Day: _____

How well did I:

	Not very well	OK	Great
• Pay attention?	1	2	3
• Discuss the topic and give examples?	1	2	3
• Think of personal examples?	1	2	3
• Practice role playing the skill?	1	2	3
• Work on my personal goal?	1	2	3
• Give others feedback?	1	2	3
• Set goals and complete a contract?	1	2	3

Student's Signature: _____

Leader's Signature: _____

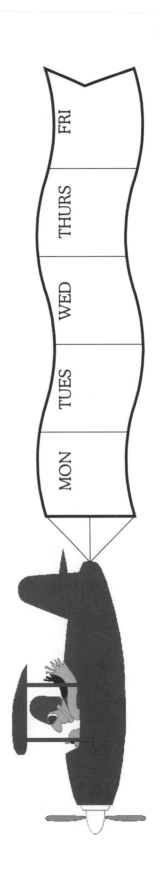

Flying High With Social Skills

Part I—Social Skills Concepts

**I was caught
doing a
SUPER JOB!**

Awarded to:

_____

**I was caught
doing a
SUPER JOB!**

Awarded to:

_____

**I was caught
doing a
SUPER JOB!**

Awarded to:

_____

**I was caught
doing a
SUPER JOB!**

Awarded to:

_____

**I was caught
doing a
SUPER JOB!**

Awarded to:

_____

**I was caught
doing a
SUPER JOB!**

Awarded to:

_____

**I was caught
doing a
SUPER JOB!**

Awarded to:

_____

**I was caught
doing a
SUPER JOB!**

Awarded to:

_____

**I was caught
doing a
SUPER JOB!**

Awarded to:

_____

**I was caught
doing a
SUPER JOB!**

Awarded to:

_____

**I was caught
doing a
SUPER JOB!**

Awarded to:

_____

**I was caught
doing a
SUPER JOB!**

Awarded to:

_____

Classroom Bank Points

Name	MON	TUE	WED	THUR	FRI	Total

Chapter 4

Leading a Social Skills Group

There are no hard and fast rules for conducting social skills groups for Tough Kids, but if there were, the first would be to **have fun**! Social skills are about getting along with other people, so groups that focus on these skills should naturally be enjoyable to you and to the Tough Kids with whom you work. Show Tough Kids, through your actions and words, that using good social skills can be fun and have naturally rewarding consequences. Do not be afraid to use humor, make jokes, and laugh with students in groups; after all, a good sense of humor suggests good social skills!

In this chapter, suggestions for conducting social skills groups will be presented. The procedures that will be described have been used successfully in small groups of four to eight students and in classrooms of up to 35 students. Entire schools have also used the procedures in comprehensive, school-wide social skills training programs. The basic competencies required of social skills group leaders will be discussed in order to assist you in preparing for the task of conducting groups. In addition, the basic procedures used in the training program are presented. Part II of this book ("Training Session Outlines") helps you put it all together by providing outlines for conducting social skills training sessions in small groups, classrooms, or schools.

> "Formal coursework in group dynamics and social development is not critical to being an effective group leader."

Leader Skills

Leading a children's social skills group—whether it be a small group, classroom, or school-wide application—is not always an easy task. There are a number of important leader skills needed to conduct groups effectively. These skills can be broken into two groups: **knowledge** about social skills and behavior management, and **personal skills** that allow you to get along well with others.

Knowledge Base

To conduct social skills groups for Tough Kids, adult leaders must understand several topics. First, knowledge in the areas of group dynamics, member participation, and social skills development is essential. This includes skills for encouraging Tough Kids to participate in group discussions. Formal coursework in group dynamics and social development is not critical to being an effective group leader. However, some resources should be helpful in developing a knowledge base in these areas. A particularly good reference is *Groups: Process and Practice*, (1992) by Marianne and Gerald Corey.

Second, it is useful to know about social development, the social problems of Tough Kids, and behavior management techniques. Chapter 1 reviews some of the difficulties that Tough Kids experience with classmates, peers, and adults. Effective behavioral management techniques will also be important to keep control of students in social skills group sessions. These procedures are thoroughly covered in *The Tough Kid Book: Practical Classroom Management Strategies*, (1992) by Ginger Rhode, William R. Jenson, and H. Kenton Reavis.

Personal Skills

A number of personal skills are important in order to coordinate and conduct groups. Especially important are patience, organization, a sense of humor, and an ability to respond quickly. Good observational skills will also be of assistance when trying to understand each group of students. You will learn quickly that in some groups, many different behaviors and temperaments will be present. In other groups, however, the group takes on a personality all its own due to the commonality of students and similarity in their behaviors. Your ability to identify key behavioral elements of your group as a whole, as well as individual mannerisms of specific students, will help increase the success of social skills training. For example, if you are conducting a group for eight Tough Kids (heaven help you . . .) you will want to set firm expectations and limits about what is acceptable in the group sessions early on. (By the way, it is usually beneficial to balance your group with students who demonstrate varying levels of problems, and not have all extremely challenging students in one group.)

It will also be important to clarify activities that will be required of the students outside of the group (e.g., homework and practice). You will also have to **speak a certain language** with Tough Kids to convey to them that you understand them, and to invite them to trust you. In general, the more you can use words that students use (within limits, of course), the more credibility you will earn.

When conducting groups for Tough Kids, good organizational skills are important for a number of reasons. They will help manage the group from start to finish, and they will be important in making sense out of information and observations that accumulate over time. It is recommended that you carefully follow the outlines and timelines provided in Part II of this book to maintain consistency and focus (they have been tested and demonstrated to be effective; see Sheridan, Dee, Morgan, McCormick, & Walker, 1996), as well as to ensure that all important aspects of the group are given sufficient time and attention.

Although these personal skills are somewhat intangible leader qualities, they are essential in keeping the group members engaged and attentive. Students seem to benefit most from the social skills group (whatever its size) when it is highly structured, and when leaders use a certain degree of humor and exude a relaxed but energetic attitude.

Group Procedures

The social skills group meets for ten or more weekly sessions, which are 60 minutes in length. The procedures used in social skills training for students are identical from week to week. They include a weekly review, instruction of a new skill, modeling, role play, feedback, and goal setting. Skill sheets (or cue cards), which list the steps of the weekly social skill, can be provided to remind students of the steps and provide them with something that can be taken with them after group time.

If time permits, a semi-structured play time can be included to allow students to use their newly learned skills. During this play time, students play freely, or they can be presented with a challenging group game that might stir up conflict and require them to solve social problems. Ideally, this type of scenario might encourage the students to engage in mutual problem solving and to select socially appropriate options. This play time can also provide an important opportunity for leaders to observe Tough Kids' behaviors and attempts (or lack thereof) to use the social skills being covered in the group. If students fail to use the skills or use them ineffectively, leaders can then prompt them to use the skills in a more successful manner.

A general outline for the weekly student sessions is presented in Box 4-1. This format has been proven to be very useful for conducting the social skills training sessions, whether they are held in small groups or classrooms. This outline provides the necessary structure for leaders to cover important activities, but it is also flexible enough to allow leaders to individualize the group format if necessary. The following is a discussion of each of the primary components of group sessions: discussion, modeling, role play, feedback, and goal setting.

Discussion of Skills

Some time should be spent at the beginning of each group session discussing students' homework, the skill of the week, the skill's

---

Box 4-1

Social Skills Training Outline

I. **Review of Previous Skill**

    A. Discuss homework and behavioral contracts.

    B. Reinforce those who brought back homework.

    C. Discuss importance of bringing back homework.

    D. Reinforce those who met goals, if specified on contract.

II. **Teach Weekly Skill**

    A. Provide rationale/discussion for skill.

    B. Teach steps, with "cue cards."

    C. Elicit examples and real life situations from group members.

    D. Model skill with student or co-leader.

    E. Have students role play skill in front of group or in small groups.

    F. Provide ongoing feedback.

III. **Group Process**

    A. Review performance of group members.

    B. Provide feedback and prompt peer feedback.

    C. Vote on adherence to group rules and personal goals.

    D. Provide reinforcers to those who earned them.

IV. **Socialization Time** (time permitting)

    A. Allow students to interact in a semi-structured play time.

    B. Prompt students to use skills learned in the group.

V. **Establishing Behavioral Programs** (Contracts)

    A. Complete homework sheet and contract with each student.

    B. Discuss how and when goal can be attained.

    C. Decide on contingencies for successful completion of goal.

---

importance in everyday life, and examples of situations when the skill was or was not used by students. The discussion at the early part of the group is important because it sets the stage for the rest of the session. In general, this time should be spent clarifying what is meant by the skill. For example, what does solving problems entail?

> "The more you can involve students throughout the entire session the better!"

A step-by-step format is helpful when presenting a new skill because it helps students remember specific and discrete steps for a particular skill. A poster, much like the ones included in Part II of this book, is important to use while presenting the skill as well as afterwards. For example, you can gain participation of several students by asking them to read steps and tell in their own words what they mean. Hanging the poster on the chalkboard is helpful while students are role playing and giving each other feedback. After the group session is over, the poster can be placed in a central spot in the classroom, such as a bulletin board, so that students are continually reminded of the steps they are to practice.

Several examples should be obtained from students about weekly social skills. For example, Bubba could be asked to think about and report on experiences he has had when the skill of **using self-control** might have been appropriate, or when he could apply it in the future. Older students might be asked to write down on a sheet of paper or an index card a description of one time that they should have used the target skill. This is important for at least two reasons. First, it encourages students to come up with at least one example or experience from their own lives when the skill could have been useful. Second, the cards can be collected and used during modeling and role playing later in the group.

The opening discussion should be relatively fast paced and brief (no longer than ten minutes). If it lasts too long, the students (especially Tough Kids) will probably become distracted and lose interest. Once that happens, it will be very difficult to get them focused for the remainder of the group.

Modeling

After discussing the skill to be practiced, leaders model (demonstrate) the behavior for students. Modeling involves seven steps, which are outlined in How To Box 4-1. Modeling is important because it demonstrates **exactly** what you mean with each step of the skill, and what these skills "look like" when practiced. When modeling, it is useful to use an actual situation that was suggested by a group member during the initial discussion. This will make the situation relevant and illustrate how the skills can be used in the students' own situations. Keep in mind that students will often mirror the example shown by leaders (almost identically in some situations) when they are given the opportunity to role play. This increases the importance of using students' actual experiences and modeling for them an appropriate response to those situations.

In some groups, you may want to have a leader model the skill with a student from the group, rather than with a co-leader. This can be especially important when your group is comprised of distractible, inattentive, or otherwise fidgety students. The more you can involve students throughout the entire session, the better! This strategy is also helpful when working with students who might be reluctant to role play. Being involved with a leader in modeling may help such students become more comfortable with this type of performance, and ultimately become more comfortable with role play.

Some group leaders like using both **positive** and **negative** models (some call them examples and nonexamples) during social skills training. This procedure involves demonstrating both how the skill **should** look and also how it **should not** look. Sometimes negative models add humor to

How To Box 4-1

Steps of Modeling

1. Define the skill and discuss its importance.

2. Discuss situations when the skill can be used in students' lives, especially in situations where peers are involved.

3. Select a situation suggested by a student. Ask a co-leader or the student who provided the situation to complete the example with you.

4. Instruct students to observe you demonstrating the skill with the co-leader or student. Tell students to pay special attention to the skill steps so they can provide feedback.

5. Complete the modeling example by either demonstrating all of the skill steps, or leaving one or two important steps out. When demonstrating the steps of solving problems (and skills using similar cognitive steps), use **think aloud** procedures by stating your thoughts regarding the problem, choices, and consequences.

6. Ask students to report what they observed you doing, with emphasis on the skill steps. If all skill steps were shown, state how they were demonstrated.

    If some skill steps were not shown, or were shown incorrectly, make sure this is pointed out by a group member or yourself. Repeat the modeled example, this time completing all of the skill steps. Ask the group again to report what they observed.

7. Make sure students understand the skill steps and what they entail. If necessary, repeat a skill modeling exercise using a different situation.

the group and encourage Tough Kids to participate (they seem attracted to these kinds of modeling examples!). If you choose to demonstrate a poor example of a skill, be sure to follow that with a good example so that the final model that the students see demonstrates an appropriate use of the skill.

Role Play

Role play is a major component of the group sessions. During role play, students are faced with a situation that requires them to use the skill being taught, and they are instructed to apply that skill to the situation. As with modeling, it is vitally important to use Tough Kids' own examples of real life situations to role play. This will make the experience more relevant and might increase their understanding of how the skills can be used from day to day.

There are a number of ways that relevant and meaningful situations can be incorporated into the group role plays. First, ways to encourage students to provide examples in the group discussion have already been outlined. As suggested, these situations can be demonstrated through role play. An important ingredient to role plays is making the recreation as close to the actual situation as possible, so ask the student who gives the example to report who was present, what everyone was doing, and what led up to the problem. Second, examples of problem situations can also be obtained from teachers and parents using a form such as the one presented in Figure 4-1. The form is helpful because it includes sections for observations regarding Tough Kids' difficulties, as well as specific situations that have occurred.

A third strategy to enhance the situations used in role plays is to ask students to pretend they are going to write a book or a movie. The movie will be about themselves and other kids at school. Also their movie should have something to do with the skill that is being taught (e.g., solving problems). In setting up the role plays, ask students to report: (1) Who was there? (2) What was happening? and (3) What should they do? This can lead directly into a role play where Tough Kids act out the alternative they choose to respond to the situation. The structure this format provides is particularly good for students who have problems taking ownership for problems ("I do not have any problems!"), and for those who appear reserved or uncomfortable about acting out problems they have experienced.

There are ten steps for role playing. These steps are outlined in How To Box 4-2. When setting up role plays, try to pair students who do not have an extensive history of fighting or other problems with each other, especially in role plays that call for solving problems or using self-control when in arguments or provoked. Because one individual will have the role of instigator, this situation could potentially backfire and you might be faced with a major problem on your hands! (By the way, the group rule of "Stay in your own space" also pertains to role plays. This means that students should not be allowed to make any type of physical contact with each other during these situations, even if they call for some type of confrontation.) It is also advised not to pair best friends or students who often play or get silly together. These kinds of pairs often have a hard time taking role-play situations seriously and may try to get the other off track or accelerate the other's inappropriate behaviors.

It is a rare situation where a student performs the role play perfectly the first time. For example, one can predict that Bubba will quickly show his true colors in role plays with sharp comebacks, name calling, and other impulsive actions. Rather than allowing him to continue in a role-play situation (often getting himself into more trouble with a peer rather than learning how to stay out of it), stop him as soon as he demonstrates an inappropriate action (such as failing to think before responding). A simple "Cut!"—as though you were a director in his movie—is useful to stop the action. Ask the other group members how they think he is doing and what he should try instead. The role play can then be performed again and continued until

Figure 4-1

Social Situations for Role Play

Student's Name: _____ Date: _____

Your Name: _____

This student is involved in a social skills group where he/she is learning how to improve his/her relationships with others. We would like your help in making the group a positive experience for this student. Please take a few minutes of your time and complete the following questions. We will use this information during the group as examples and situations for the student to work through. In this way, the things we do in group should be much more meaningful for him/her. Thank you!

Describe any general concerns you have about this student's friendships and social skills. In other words, generally speaking, how does this student get along with his/her peers?

Describe at least three specific problematic situations that recently occurred between this student and other students. Be specific with your examples.

1._____
_____
_____
_____

2._____
_____
_____
_____

3._____
_____
_____
_____

Bubba gets into another bind. It is important to stop him when he has problems so that he does not continue to practice mistakes. This type of immediate feedback (stopping a social interaction while it is going on) can be very instructional for Bubba, who might not otherwise think about how important each of his actions are when practicing new skills. If feedback is not provided until the end of role play, Bubba will not be forced to analyze each component behavior (both appropriate and unadaptive) that occurred throughout. Rather, he might deduce that the sequence of behaviors resulted in an acceptable end result (as it sometimes does), so what he did must be acceptable.

Feedback

Beyond immediate feedback during role plays, there are many other important types of feedback when conducting social skills training with Tough Kids. A formal opportunity to provide feedback occurs at the end of the group. Also, many informal opportunities for feedback are

How To Box 4-2

Steps for Role Playing

1. Present the skill of the week, using a poster and cue cards for students. Model the skill at least once for the students.

2. Ask students to think about situations they have experienced in which they could have used the skill of the week. This can be done with a statement such as, "What is one time that you could have used these steps with friends?"

   For the first few weeks of social skills training, students may feel uncomfortable role playing. A more indirect approach might be necessary. For example, you might consider asking students to pretend that they are going to write a true story or a movie about themselves at school (or home) with other kids. The story or movie should incorporate the skill of the week.

3. Select a volunteer (Student 1) to be involved in a role play. If no student volunteers, encourage an individual student and offer to be in the role play with him/her.

4. Ask the student to state: (1) who is involved in the situation, (2) what is happening, and (3) what he/she will do.

5. Select a volunteer (Student 2) to role play with the student, acting as another person in the situation.

6. Instruct the other students in the group ("observers") to carefully watch the role play, keeping in mind the skill steps in order to provide feedback after the performance.

7. Make sure the situation is fully developed to allow both the group members and the role play participants (especially Student 2) to understand what is happening.

8. Begin the role play with a quick phrase such as, "Action!" or "Go ahead!" If students are slow to respond, prompt them directly with instructions on how to start.

9. Watch the role play carefully to make sure that students respond appropriately. Do not allow any physical contact or verbal abuse. If Student 1 uses his/her steps appropriately and effectively, allow him/her to complete the role play. If he/she fails to use the appropriate skill steps (that is, if he/she begins to use inappropriate or ineffective behaviors):

   - Stop him/her immediately (use a quick phrase such as "Cut" or "Time out").

   - Ask the observers to give Student 1 feedback about his/her performance (see guidelines for eliciting and providing peer feedback in How To Box 4-3).

   - Provide a positive comment about the student's performance, followed by constructive feedback about the behavior of concern (e.g., "You are doing a good job using eye contact. . . , try to take a deep breath and think about your choices instead of arguing with Tommy.").

   - Instruct the student to perform the role play again, starting at the point at which he/she had difficulty. Allow him/her to complete the role play appropriately, and encourage peer feedback at the end.

10. Continue selecting volunteers and following the same procedures until all students have had an opportunity to role play, or until time runs out.

built into the group. In general, both positive and constructive feedback should be used.

A basic form of **positive feedback** is praise, otherwise known as positive reinforcement.

How To Box 4-3

Increasing the Effectiveness of Peer Feedback

You cannot assume that students will know how to give each other helpful feedback during group skills training. During the first or second week, spend some time discussing the importance of feedback, how to make it effective, and how and when to use it inside and outside of the group meetings. Below are some suggestions for presenting feedback to the students. If students have difficulty following the steps of giving feedback, devote one social skills session to the skill.

1. Discuss the importance of being good observers of each other's behaviors. This can be approached by reminding students that they can learn a lot from each other, and that they can help each other learn new ways of getting along.

2. Instruct group members that an important part of the social skills group is being able to give each other ideas about what they are doing well (behaviors that other kids like), and ideas about what they are not doing well (actions that other students may not like, or that could be changed).

3. Teach students five steps for giving feedback:

   • Use a nice voice.
   • Look at the person.
   • Wait for an appropriate time.
   • Start by saying something positive (something that the person is doing well).
   • Provide a suggestion for changing a particular behavior.

4. Encourage students to use statements that are common in their vocabulary. This increases the chance that they will use similar statements in other situations. It also increases the chance that the receiver of the feedback will take it seriously. For example, a statement such as "That was great the way you kept your cool when Rex tried to get into a fight!" is probably going to be more meaningful than a statement such as "I like the way you used self-control." (The latter statement might be used in groups, but it probably will not be as effective in real life as the former.)

5. Model what giving feedback looks like, using several examples.

6. Have students practice by giving feedback to leaders following modeling examples.

7. Suggest that students provide feedback during discussions, role plays, and other times during group. When necessary, help students provide appropriate feedback statements by reminding them of the steps involved.

8. Discuss opportunities that students have outside of the group—on the playground, in the classroom, on the school bus—when they can give feedback using the techniques learned in the group.

9. Throughout all group sessions, provide ample opportunities for students to give each other feedback.

When working with Tough Kids, do not hesitate to use a lot of verbal praise for any and all behaviors that are desirable, such as volunteering to participate, paying attention, and following the appropriate social skills steps. The co-leader in a group is often in a good position to give individual positive feedback to students without disrupting the group. Keep in mind that in some situations, such as when a Tough Kid is doing an outstanding job participating or paying attention, you may want to praise him/her publicly. This type of recognition can go a long way in bolstering his/her self-esteem and helping other students see him/her in a positive light.

Constructive feedback should be provided when students' behaviors are inappropriate or when skill attempts are imperfect. Constructive feedback is meant to give Tough Kids suggestions for improving behavior or performance, but it is delivered in a supportive and nonthreatening way. It usually starts with a positive comment—"You did a great job suggesting to Jesse that you take turns choosing what to play at recess"—and is then followed with a direct and specific suggestion for making the attempt more effective—"It would work even better if you use eye contact when speaking with Jesse."

Positive and constructive feedback from group leaders is an important part of social skills training and should be used often and sincerely. Not only does it get the point across to the student to whom it is directed, but it also models the social skill of "giving feedback" for students in the group. In other words, your frequent and effective feedback can teach Tough Kids and other students how to tell others what is appropriate and inappropriate about their behaviors.

Early on in the group (in the first few sessions) most of the feedback will be given by leaders. However, as the training sessions progress, it is important to begin providing opportunities for students to give feedback to each other. This can occur during the group discussion, during and after role plays, and at the end of the group session. Peer feedback is a potentially powerful aspect of the group, because what Tough Kids hear from peers is often more important than what they hear from adults. It is also an important skill for students to learn since it can help them in many social situations. Suggestions for increasing the effectiveness of peer feedback are listed in How To Box 4-3.

Keep in mind that any situation where you as a leader are tempted to provide feedback is a situation where a peer might also provide feedback. Before giving feedback yourself, you might consider asking another group member what he/she can suggest.

Toward the end of each group session, take five to seven minutes for general feedback to each student. Keeping with the philosophy that students take feedback from their peers seriously, encourage students to tell each other about their performance and behaviors during group time. Because this is not something that students will do naturally, they will need to be told and shown how to give feedback appropriately (in fact, you might even want to conduct an entire lesson devoted to this important skill). We use a format that encourages students to say one good thing about the other person first, and then one thing that he or she should try to do differently. The student giving feedback should use eye contact and talk directly to the person, using his or her name. The ideas for improvement should not simply be general comments; rather, they should tell the student receiving feedback exactly what to try. The statements should also use words or phrases that are common to students' everyday language and not overly formal or superficial. For example, the following is a good feedback statement: "Bubba, you really participated well today. Maybe you should try to relax a little bit and not clench your fists when asking other kids questions." Compare this to a less effective feedback statement: "You participated but seemed really uptight."

Goal Setting

Goal setting is a strategy that students can use to gain control over their relationships and behaviors with friends. It is very important because it conveys clear expectations and concrete plans for Tough Kids to practice and use their social skills outside of the group setting. In goal setting, students are helped to set specific goals for their social behaviors, to evaluate their progress towards those goals, and to follow up with revised goals as necessary. Specifically, each week at the end of the social skills group, students set a goal for using the newly learned skill. If encouraged to set goals related to the social skill of the week, students will be frequently reminded of it and be much more inclined to use it in specific, real life situations.

Suggested guidelines for setting goals with Tough Kids are presented in How To Box 4-4, with examples of appropriate and inappropriate goal statements in Box 4-2. When goal setting, the first goal you set with a student should be one that you are fairly certain the student can accomplish. In other words, set students up for success, not failure. For example, Tina, a very shy and timid nine-year old, may set a goal to start three conversations with classmates during one recess period, even though she has never started even one in the past. For Tina, it would be inappropriate to expect that she could be successful in meeting this goal. It is probable that she is setting herself up for failure. A better goal would be: "I will start one conversation with Anne at recess today." Similarly, a goal such as "I will give 30 compliments to classmates today" is probably not manageable. A student will probably not achieve this goal because it is close to impossible, not because he/she does not possess the skills to give compliments.

As with all other social skills, it is important to encourage and expect students to make their own decisions about what goals to set for themselves. After all, we cannot expect that students (especially Tough Kids) will accept what we suggest unless they believe that it is personally appropriate and worthwhile. Also, they will be much likelier to work toward meeting their goals if they truly believe that they are important. You might think that Bubba, for example, should set a goal such as "I will use the steps of self-control at least one time at every lunch recess." On the other hand, he might prefer a goal that deals with using self-control at baseball practice. It is likely that if you force him to accept a goal for recess, he will rebel and have a hard time at both recess

and at baseball practice. As long as students' preferences are acceptable within appropriate limits, allow them to set their own goals and make their own decisions for action.

Sometimes students will have unrealistic expectations about what is an appropriate goal, or they will state goals in ways that make it difficult for them to be successful. Although it is helpful to encourage students to set their own goals as much as possible, it is also necessary to help them set goals that are feasible. Suggested steps for goal setting are in How To Box 4-5 on page 89.

A formal **contract system** is essential for goal-setting. The contracts serve as agreements with Tough Kids about how they will use their skills in the upcoming week. Good contracts include all of the details of the plan so that Tough Kids know exactly what is expected of them.

"Sign all copies . . . . "

At a minimum, contracts should include: (1) The social goals students set for themselves (e.g., "I will tell Stuart that I do not like it when he cuts in front of me in the cafeteria line during lunch," or "I will use a calm voice when talking on the playground."); (2) The time frame for completing the goal (e.g., "every day this week during lunch recess."); (3) How students will keep track of the behavior (e.g., points, stickers); (4) What will be earned (e.g., Mystery Motivators, ten minutes of free time in class on a Friday afternoon, lunch with the principal, etc.); and (5) When the rewards will be earned (e.g., every day after recess, at the end of each school day, every

How To Box 4-4

Setting Goals With Tough Kids

1. **Help students choose goals that they will probably be successful in meeting.** In general, the first goals set with students should require them to do things they have already done successfully. Later goals can require, in very small steps, that they begin to practice new skills. In this way, by the time students attempt more difficult goals, they will have been successful with previous, simpler goals.

2. **Encourage students to make goals very specific.** Goals should indicate important information of **what**, **when**, **where**, **with whom**, and **how** the behavior will be demonstrated. For example, a goal such as "At school this morning I will tell Paul in a calm voice that I feel sad when he teases me in front of the other kids," is very specific and concrete. On the other hand, a goal such as "I will express my feelings to a friend today," is overly vague and nonspecific. It does not provide enough concrete direction to students, and they may not meet the goal because they are confused or unsure of exactly what to do.

3. **Ensure that goals students select are ones over which they have control.** At times, students might set goals that require some action on the part of someone else. For example, to meet the goal of "I will go to the movies with Stephanie on Saturday,"

Stephanie must be available and willing to go. (It also requires that the students have permission from their parents, and that they can pay for the movie!) A better goal would be, "If my parents say it's okay, I will ask Stephanie to go to the movies with me on Saturday." This goal is something students can accomplish on their own.

4. **Help students select goals that tell them what to do, rather than what not to do.** Goals that emphasize what to do will help students choose more appropriate ways to handle problems with friends. For example, the goal "I will ask Fred if I can play soccer with him at recess," is better than "I won't stand alone at recess." The first goal gives the student specific directions about what to do instead of standing alone.

5. **Decide with students how to keep track and evaluate attainment of goals.** When setting goals, discuss with students how they will know if they have met their goals. Set up a time with each student to discuss his/her attempts at meeting his/her goal. One easy way to do this is to determine a timeline as part of the student's goal statement. For example, the student may set a goal such as "I will call Michael on the phone by Tuesday evening," which can then be easily reviewed Wednesday morning.

Friday, at the next group session, etc.). Obviously, the details specified depend largely on the person with whom each Tough Kid enters into the contract. For example, if Bubba's classroom teacher agrees to work on a social skills contract with him, classroom-based reinforcers (e.g., free time on a Friday afternoon) are possible, and

checks can occur almost on a daily basis. If the school psychologist is conducting the social skills group for Bubba and other Tough Kids, he/she would specify and deliver the reinforcers (e.g., a Mystery Motivator or Spinner move) in the next group session.

Box 4-2

Examples of Goal Statements

Following are some examples of appropriate and inappropriate goals that may be set by students. Two examples corresponding to each "rule" are provided.

Rule	Goal	Better Goal
1. **Successful**	I will play with Jackie every recess period.	I will play with Jackie at least two times this week.
	I will compliment Peter ten times tomorrow.	I will give Peter two compliments before Friday.
2. **Specific**	I will be nice to my friends this week.	I will give Ian and Mark one compliment each before Wednesday.
	I will be a good friend.	I will invite Jane to my house one day before Sunday.
3. **Control**	I will make friends with the new girl, Sarah.	I will ask Sarah to play with me at recess tomorrow.
	I will play football with Jared everyday.	I will ask Jared if I can play football with him twice before Wednesday.
4. **Tells What to Do**	I will not fight with my friends.	I will use problem solving with friends twice this week.
	I will not get mad when I can't play on the team.	I will accept "No" when asking if I can be on the team.

Sample contracts are presented in Figure 4-2. These contracts can easily be reproduced on the reverse side of students' homework sheets (Figure 4-3) to decrease the number of papers that Tough Kids will have to manage. You will notice that a chart is included on the *Homework Sheet* to give Tough Kids a simple form on which they can keep track each day of their use of the target skill.

At times Tough Kids' goals will be to use the weekly skill on a daily basis (e.g., during recess); other weeks their goals might be to use the skill in specific situations that are likely to be problematic (e.g., when being teased or left out of a game). Regardless of how goals are stated, it will be useful for Tough Kids to keep track on their *Homework Charts* every time they are able to successfully use the target skill. This kind of information is helpful for students to see the progress they are making in using weekly skills in a variety of situations, and it will be useful to you as the leader to gauge how effectively they are incorporating the skills into their daily lives. In group sessions, you might ask students to report on occurrences that were reported on their *Homework Sheets*. Each student can share with the group what happened, who was involved, what he/she did, and what the outcome was.

Positive Reinforcement

When trying to increase any desired behavior, positive reinforcement is a must. Many short- and long-term positive reinforcers are used in social skills groups. Reinforcers are provided to students for their performance within the group sessions, as well as for practicing the skills outside the training setting.

First, a great deal of **positive verbal and non-verbal reinforcement** should be provided to students during group training sessions. This should come from the leaders, as well as from other students. Praise and encouragement can be conveyed through the use of high fives, smiles, and pats on the back. Verbally, it is important to be specific about what you are reinforcing and to reinforce socially appropriate behaviors as soon as they occur. The **IFEED** rules, discussed in *The Tough Kid Book: Practical Classroom Management Strategies* (1992), are appropriate for praising social skills. In general, the rules state that when verbally reinforcing students, make sure that your statements are **I**mmediate, **F**requent, and **E**nthusiastic. Also, it is important that leaders use **E**ye contact and **D**escribe the exact behaviors they are praising. Box 4-3 gives examples of each of these rules as they pertain to social skills.

❓ How To Box 4-5

Steps for Goal Setting

1. Make sure that the student is ready to set a goal.

2. Help the student identify the problem, explore possible solutions, and choose the best one. When the student decides on a solution, it can be stated as a goal.

3. Ask the student to state the goal using an "I-statement" (e.g., "I will start a conversation with Eli today.").

4. Make sure that the goal is **specific**, **manageable**, and **positive**. In other words, the goal should describe one specific behavior (e.g., "invite a friend to play") so that the student will know exactly what to do in order to meet it. It should be a goal that the student has control over and that he/she will probably be successful in meeting. It should tell the student what to do, rather than what not to do.

5. Write down the goal. Include when the student will attempt the goal (e.g., tomorrow afternoon), where (e.g., on the playground), and with whom (e.g., "with Mary").

6. Decide on how to measure completion of the goal. Include a time frame for the student to complete the goal (e.g., "by Monday"), and the number of times a behavior must occur (e.g., "three times this week") for completion of the goal.

Figure 4-2

Figure 4-3

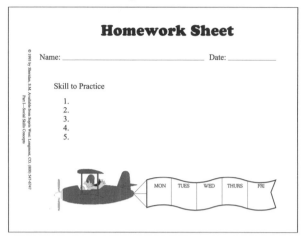

Homework Sheet

Name: _____   Date: _____

Skill to Practice
1.
2.
3.
4.
5.

| MON | TUES | WED | THURS | FRI |

Figure 4-4

JOHN'S

Recording on Tape Recorder 30 min. After School

15 Minutes Free Time

10 min. Choice of Game With Friend

First in Line

Candy Treat

Surprise Box of Things To Do

20 Extra Bank Points

Sit Anywhere In Class

Get to Pass Out Papers to Class

SPINNER

The more positive and upbeat you can make the social skills sessions, the more likely students will look forward to the sessions, take them seriously, and begin to expect others to do the same. Also, lots of positive attention might encourage students to begin to support each other by providing praise and encouragement.

Another reinforcement system used in social skills training makes use of **weekly tangible reinforcers** that students earn if they meet their goal for the week. The details of the weekly reinforcement program can be laid out in a behavioral contract, which has already been described. Additionally, various exciting formats can be used to deliver the weekly reinforcers. For example, a **Spinner** system can be used where students earn a spin if they meet their behavioral goals. Several possible rewards are posted on a spinner card, such as the one in Figure 4-4.

The Spinner is divided into several sections of various sizes. High interest rewards, such as free time on a Friday afternoon or five extra minutes of recess, are posted on the smallest sections of the spinner. Other reinforcers, such as

being the first in line for lunch or collecting class papers, are placed on larger sections. This increases the chance that lower interest reinforcers will be landed on more often than higher interest ones, keeping students motivated to earn spins in anticipation of landing on a small section. Students should help identify the different reinforcers to include on the Spinner. They can also rank them from most to least exciting to ensure that the highest valued rewards are placed on the smallest segments of the Spinner.

GOOD JOB!

WAY TO GO!

"Subtlety is Lost on Tough Kids"

Box 4-3

Examples of IFEED Rules for Social Skills

Immediately: The "I" stands for reinforcing the student immediately. The longer the teacher waits to reinforce a student, the less effective the reinforcer will be. This is particularly true of younger students or students with severe disabilities. For example, reinforcer effectiveness will be limited if the student has to wait until the end of the week to receive it.

Frequently: The "F" stands for frequently reinforcing a student. It is especially important to frequently reinforce when a student is learning a new behavior or skill. If reinforcers are not given frequently enough, the student may not produce enough of a new behavior for it to become well established. The standard rule is three or four positive reinforcers for every one negative consequence (including negative verbal comments) the teacher delivers. If, in the beginning, there is a great deal of inappropriate behavior to which the teacher must attend, positive reinforcement and recognition of appropriate behavior must be increased accordingly to maintain the desired three or four positives to each negative. The reinforcer can be a simple social reinforcer such as, "Good job. You finished your math assignment."

Enthusiasm: The first "E" stands for enthusiasm in the delivery of the reinforcer. It is easy to simply hand an edible reinforcer to a student; it takes more effort to pair it with an enthusiastic comment. Modulation in the voice and excitement with a congratulatory air conveys that the student has done something important. For most teachers, this seems artificial at first. However, with practice enthusiasm makes the difference between a reinforcer delivered in a drab, uninteresting way to one that indicates that something important has taken place in which the teacher is interested.

Eye Contact: It is also important for the teacher to look the student in the eyes when giving a reinforcer, even if the student is not looking at him/her. Like enthusiasm, eye contact suggests that a student is special and has the teacher's undivided attention. Over time, eye contact may become reinforcing in and of itself.

Describe the Behavior: "D" stands for describing the behavior that is being reinforced. The younger the student or the more severely disabled, the more important it is to describe the appropriate behavior that is being reinforced. Teachers often assume that students know what it is they are doing right that has resulted in the delivery of reinforcement. However, this is often not the case. The student may not know why reinforcement is being delivered or think that it is being delivered for some behavior other than what the teacher intended to reinforce. Even if the student does know what behavior is being reinforced, describing it is important.

For one thing, describing the behavior highlights and emphasizes the behavior the teacher wishes to reinforce. Second, if the behavior has several steps, describing it helps to review the specific expectations for the student. An example is, "Wow, you got yourself dressed—look at you! You have your socks on, your shoes are laced, your pants are on with a belt, and your shirt has all the buttons fastened and is tucked in." This is much more effective than saying, "Good dressing."

From *The Tough Kid Book: Practical Classroom Management Strategies* (p. 41) by Rhode, Jenson, & Reavis, 1993, Longmont, CO: Sopris West.

"Everybody Loves a Party"

Alternatively, **Mystery Motivators** can be used to deliver weekly reinforcers. Mystery Motivators are described in *The Tough Kid Book* and *The Tough Kid Tool Box*, and provide fun and interesting methods to keep students excited about the group. There are many variations for using Mystery Motivators. For instance, they have been successfully used in conjunction with **grab bags**. Prior to the first group session, leaders prepare a grab bag filled with small and inexpensive objects that might be reinforcing to students in the group. Examples include sports cards, cans of sugar-free soda, pencils, small balls, or tokens for a local video arcade.

Leaders prepare a Mystery Motivator envelope (see Figure 4-5) that contains individual slips of paper, each of which has the names of all available reinforcers written with invisible ink. Special markers are available that will expose the invisible ink and indicate the reward earned from the grab bag. If a student returns his/her Homework Sheet and has met his/her goal, he/she earns the privilege of selecting a slip of paper from the Mystery Motivator envelope. He/she

Figure 4-5

then uses the special marker to expose the reward and take it from the grab bag.

A third reinforcement system utilizes a *Weekly Homework Chart* posted in the front of the room with all group participants' names listed along the left margin. The dates of group meetings are horizontally listed along the top of the chart (see Figure 4-6). Each student places a star, sticker, stamp, or some other token in the appropriate box corresponding to the day homework was returned. Alternatively, a dot-to-dot chart or *Social Skills Homework Thermometer* (see Figure 4-6) can also be used. Students connect dots or color special boxes each day they return their homework.

With any of these reinforcement systems, students can be informed that if they bring their homework back at least six out of eight days that it is assigned, they will earn a **party** and **special reward** on the last day. Items that have been used as special rewards include frozen yogurt coupons, a t-shirt decorating party, and discount movie tickets. This system is especially useful for students who may work hard and bring homework back each week, but consistently fail to meet their goals.

A fourth positive reinforcement component of social skills groups is a **group party** held during the last session. The party is conducted as an enjoyable event where leaders and students celebrate what they have accomplished. All students in the group should be allowed to participate in the party. It is helpful to provide certificates of completion and autograph scrapbooks (see

Figure 4-6

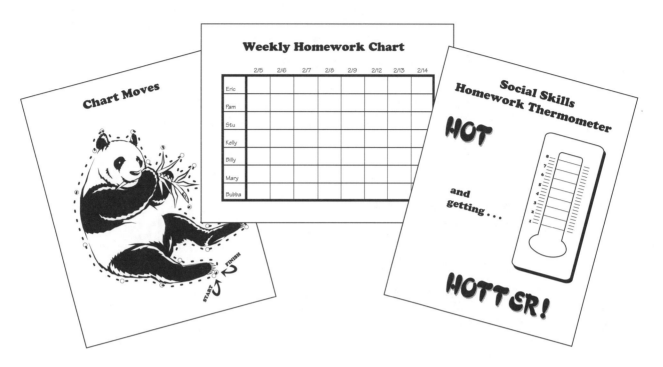

"Classroom Posters" section of this book) as a means of closure for the students. The booklets can be kept by the students following group completion as a physical reminder of social skills groups, and of the skill steps. A sample certificate is presented in Figure 4-7.

Other Program Components

Group Rules

Anyone that has ever worked with Tough Kids knows the importance of establishing rules and setting limits. Rules and limits also apply to social skills groups. You should establish rules during the first social skills training session to increase your control of the group. In general, rules should be stated in positive terms (i.e., they tell the students what to do, rather than what not to do), and there should be no more than five formal rules. Common rules that are used in social skills groups are presented in Box 4-4. A poster such as

that presented in Figure 4-8 can be used. It is recommended that the rules be posted in a central location each week and reviewed for at least the first two to four weeks as a constant reminder to Tough Kids.

One of the characteristics of Tough Kids is that they like to believe that they have some control over what they will do or what is expected of

Figure 4-7

them. Because of this, it is helpful to have them help identify group rules early on, usually on the first day of the group. Most children between the ages of 8 and 12 have experience with structured group or classroom situations where rules are common. As a result, they are generally able to draw from their experiences and develop appropriate rules for the group. It may be necessary for you to restate some suggestions to ensure that all guidelines are included in the rules, and that the rules are stated in positive terms.

Box 4-4

Rules for Social Skills Groups

The following group rules generally cover most of the behavior problems that you are likely to encounter during group sessions. Early in the first group session, have students assist in listing important rules. Make sure that each of the following rules is covered in the list the group generates.

1. **Stay in your own space.** Explain this rule to students by reminding them that they are not allowed to engage in any physical contact, including hitting, shoving, and kicking.

2. **Participate.** This means that students should involve themselves in the group by using personal examples during discussions and role plays.

3. **Take turns speaking.** Remind students that interruptions and "blurting out" are unaccepted.

4. **Speak in a nice voice.** During the group session, yelling and loud voices are not appropriate.

5. **Use nice words.** Students can help define what is meant by this rule, but should be told that name calling, swearing, and aggressive statements are not allowed.

Figure 4-8

Group Rules

1. Stay in your own space.
2. Participate.
3. Take turns speaking.
4. Speak in a nice voice.
5. Use nice words.

© 1995 by Sheridan, S.M. Available from Sopris West: Longmont, CO. (800) 547-6747
Part I—Social Skills Concepts

Personal Goals

The social skills taught in the group sessions are usually selected based on the needs of the group as a whole. The formal rules are useful for helping maintain structure and control (and hopefully your sanity). But it is often helpful to also establish personal goals for each student in the group. Because each Tough Kid is unique, the personal goals are developed to meet the individual training needs of each student. For example, Bubba might have a hard time remaining serious and participating in the group discussions. A personal goal for him one week (or until he seems to master it) might be to "Make at least three comments that are related to the group discussion."

It is recommended that personal goals be written on a chalkboard or posted in a visible place so that Tough Kids take them seriously (much like the group rules). Personal goals should be specific and concrete in order for Tough Kids to work at attaining them. Public recognition of Tough Kids' attempts to meet their personal goals is also useful. This could take the form of placing checkmarks on the chalkboard when behaviors related to the students' personal goals

Box 4-5

Examples of Personal Goals

Personal goals should be specific and individualized to the student for whom they are intended. Nevertheless, here are some examples that might be appropriate for students who display certain kinds of difficulties in group sessions. You are encouraged to think of others that may be more appropriate for your students.

Type of Student	Personal Goal
Shy/Reticent	"Use eye contact when giving feedback to others."
	"Participate at least four times."
Negative	"Use student-pleaser statements such as 'way to go' or 'I like that!'"
	"Smile when others speak to you."
Tense	"Keep hands and face relaxed."
	"Tell yourself 'It's OK!'"
Aggressive	"Keep hands and feet to yourself."
	"Use a friendly tone of voice."
Impulsive	"Count to five before raising your hand."
	"Stop and take a deep breath before speaking."

are demonstrated. In some cases, you may also want to use a system whereby checkmarks are erased for inappropriate behaviors. The checkmarks can also be tied to earning a special treat at the end of the group. Examples of personal goals are listed in Box 4-5.

It is often impossible to begin developing personal goals until the second or third week of the group session. In the first couple of weeks, leaders should observe individual students and take notes on behaviors that need attention. If necessary, it is also helpful to keep the same personal goal for two or more weeks until the student shows a firm command of it. At that point, you might develop a new personal goal but keep the original one as a **secondary goal** (written in parentheses underneath the new personal goal) to

remind the student that it is important to keep working on it.

Homework

Weekly homework is given in each social skills group session. The homework involves practicing the social skill and reporting how it went to the group the following week. Homework is tied directly to goal setting and behavioral contracts.

At the end of each session students are given a *Homework Sheet* (see Figure 4-3) that has on it the skill of the week, a list of the steps necessary to perform the skill, and a self-monitoring chart where they should keep track of their use of the skill on a daily basis. Each week students are assigned the task of using the weekly skill as appropriate. If opportunities to use the skill do not arise naturally (as some students claim), they should practice the skill with their parents or teachers to complete the assignment. Each time they use or practice the skill, they are given the task of self-monitoring their performance (e.g., with tallies, stars, or stickers) on the homework sheet. Upon returning to the social skills lesson, students should report to the group how often they used the skill (i.e., how many tallies or stars they earned), with specific details about at least one instance.

On the back of the *Homework Sheet* is the behavioral contract. As already described, the contract includes a space to record Tough Kids' weekly goals, how and when they can be achieved, what can be earned, and other details.

Videotaping

If possible, videotaping social skills groups is beneficial. This provides a permanent record of what goes on in the training sessions. Segments from videotapes can be used at a later date to

remind students of the skills they were taught and the steps for achieving them. Students not only have fun viewing themselves performing skills appropriately in role play, but it also reminds them that they know how to perform the skill; this can serve as encouragement to continue to use positive social behaviors. With parent permission, videotapes might also be shared among group leaders who can give each other feedback about how to make the group more effective or meaningful. When parents are involved in training, videotapes might be shown to parents to illustrate the skills being taught to students.

Booster Sessions

An essential aspect to the social skills training program is the inclusion of booster sessions. Booster sessions formally remind Tough Kids about appropriate social skills and encourage these skills' continued use. One or two booster sessions are conducted between 8 and 16 weeks after completion of the social skills training sessions. These sessions are included in the program to promote social skills generalization over time. In the booster sessions, you should re-emphasize the importance of all of the skills, and give students the opportunity to discuss and role play problem situations that they suggest. An outline for social skills booster sessions is presented in Part II of this book.

Generalization of Social Skills—Making It Count in the Real World

The bottom line of any program for Tough Kids, including a social skills program, is making it work in everyday life. In social skills training, this takes the form of Tough Kids using the social skills they are learning in the group in many situations and interactions with peers. To be meaningful, the skills taught in the group setting need to be applied in the "real world" when Tough Kids are playing games, having conversations, working on projects, talking on the telephone, and responding to adults' questions. Ideally, the skills  should be used not only at school (e.g., in the classroom, lunchroom, and playground), but also at home, in the grocery or toy store, during club meetings, at the park, or at the bowling alley. This is known as **generalization**.

The social skills training program uses many different strategies to promote generalization to a variety of places and situations. Concrete strategies include homework, goal setting, and behavioral contracts. These are discussed earlier in this chapter. Some other useful strategies are those that teachers, parents, and other adults can use (i.e., reinforcement, prompting, and modeling) to encourage students to use their skills in everyday situations. Follow-up booster sessions are also helpful for retaining skills.

Unfortunately, just because you have taught one or a group of Tough Kids appropriate skills for getting along with others, it does not automatically mean that they will use them in everyday situations. For example, it is very likely that Bubba will not necessarily realize that the skills he is learning in social skills training have any relevance in his daily interactions. This may be surprising, but it is true. In fact, one eight-year-old Tough Kid who recently completed one of our social skills training groups in a public school commented that he could not use problem solving skills with his neighborhood friends because they were not in the group and would not know what he was doing! This is not an unfamiliar thought process for Tough Kids, so comments like this may be fairly common. Therefore, a four-step process is suggested to encourage Tough Kids to use their new skills in their day-to-day lives: **recognize**, **reinforce**, **prompt**, and **model**. First, help Tough Kids to *recognize* situations in which the newly learned skills can be used. Second, verbally *reinforce* them every time you see them using appropriate

"Strrriiike"

social skills (e.g., "Hey! You and Hank played that card game really well together!" or "That was neat how you helped Shelly figure out the crossword puzzle!"). Third, *prompt* students to use their newly learned skills when situations arise but they don't use the skills independently (e.g., when they need to use a book that is being used by another student, or when a group of students gets into an argument about the rules of a game). Finally, *model* how to use the skills if students fail to respond appropriately to a prompt (e.g., show them how to politely ask their classmates to borrow a book, or demonstrate the steps for solving arguments). The primary components of generalization— reinforcement, prompting, and modeling—are described below. Considerations for their use are in Box 4-6.

Reinforcement

When trying to encourage Tough Kids to use social skills in daily life, it is important to reinforce all of their **attempts** at using positive social skills, and not simply those that are effective. Verbal praise and acknowledgement should be used liberally. Examples of positive reinforcement statements that can be used outside of the social skills group include: "Nice job working out that disagreement with Samantha!" "You did a great job sharing your things with Mary!" "I'm real proud of how well you played with Joey!"

Prompting

Prompting is necessary when you recognize opportunities when Tough Kids could have used positive social skills, but did not for some reason. When prompting students, approach them and make a statement reminding them of the

---

| Box 4-6 |

Generalization Techniques

Reinforcement:

Reinforce all of Tough Kids' attempts at using positive social skills, whether or not they are effective.

Reinforcement should be provided immediately, frequently, enthusiastically, with eye contact, and descriptively (see Box 4-3 for IFEED rules). Tell Tough Kids **specifically** what they did well. Rather than simply saying "Good job," try a statement such as "I liked the way you and Joey decided what to play next!"

Prompting:

Prompts should be delivered to Tough Kids in a neutral and supportive manner. They should not be demanding or demeaning.

Tough Kids may or may not respond to prompts. Stay with them until problems have been dealt with sufficiently.

Modeling:

Be sure that Tough Kids act out the steps that were modeled. It is not enough for them to simply observe you or another adult performing the skill.

Modeling should be short and specific. As always, provide positive reinforcement for all attempts Tough Kids make to use the skills after the modeling sequence.

---

social skill steps and suggest that they use them in the situation. For example, Bubba might be playing basketball with a friend and get into a dispute about rules. This is a good opportunity to use problem solving skills! If you observe a dispute or problem and Bubba fails to spontaneously use the problem solving steps, stop their play with a statement such as, "There seems to be a problem here. Now is a good time to use the problem-solving steps!" Reinforce all their attempts at solving the problem, whether or not they are effective. Other examples of prompting statements include: "I can see that there's a problem here. Let's try to use the problem-solving steps." "This is a good time to practice our steps of using self-control. Do you remember what they are?"

Modeling

Much like the modeling procedures used in the group sessions, modeling (or skill demonstration) is used when students fail to follow prompts, and when they do not seem to know how to use the steps in a particular situation. In modeling for generalization purposes, demonstrate and act out the appropriate steps for the student right in the setting and at the time that the skill is needed. The student observes and then imitates your actions. This gives the student an opportunity to observe and practice the steps in a specific problematic situation. Examples of modeling statements include: "Watch how I use the steps of joining in. After I am finished, I want you to use the same steps." "This is how to use the problem solving steps. Watch me and then you practice them."

Because one of the keys to generalization is to recognize opportunities for the students to use the skills they are learning, good observation skills on the part of leaders, teachers, and others are important. By now, you have had many opportunities to observe Tough Kids interacting with others. With generalization you will have a chance to step in while observing and help them use their skills on the spot. Steps for using generalization techniques are in How To Box 4-6. A

Figure 4-9

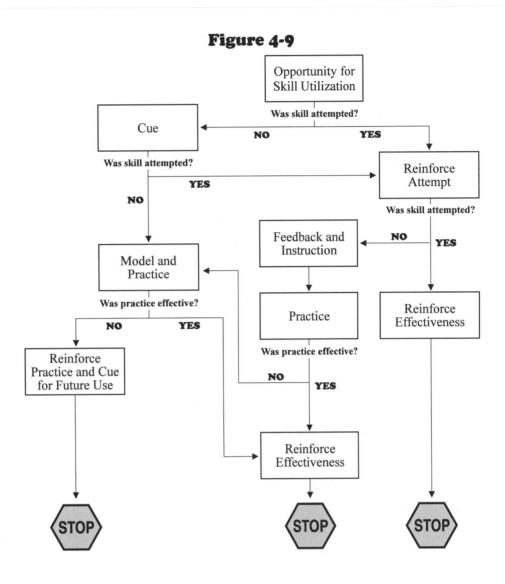

flowchart, taking you through several combinations of possible Tough Kid responses to your generalization efforts, is presented in Figure 4-9 (Jones et al., 1993).

Working With Parents and Teachers

It is strongly recommended that parents and teachers be formally involved in social skills training. For example, parents might be involved in a parent group and teachers might actually help conduct social skills training. However, this obviously will not be possible in all cases. At a minimum, ongoing input and communication between group leaders and parents and teachers is essential to successful groups.

In Chapter 2, we discussed the importance of collecting assessment information from teachers and parents. This is an important starting point, but their input and involvement should not stop there. Parents and teachers can provide important and ongoing information about the types of problems that Tough Kids are having with peers. For example, using the *Social Situations for Role Play* form presented in Figure 4-1, parents and teachers can provide group leaders with specific situations that have been problematic for students, including who was present and what happened, and these situations can be used for role plays during group time. Also, the *Weekly Social*

How To Box 4-6

Steps for Using Generalization Techniques

There are five basic steps to promoting generalization with the use of reinforcement, prompting, and modeling:

1. **Recognize** opportunities for students to use the positive social skills that were taught in social skills training.

2. **Reinforce** all attempts that students make to use skills with a statement such as, "Nice job using (or trying to use) the steps of joining in!"

3. If students fail to attempt a skill, **prompt** them with a statement such as, "This is a good time for you to try the steps of problem solving." Next:

   - If students attempt the steps after the prompt, reinforce them with a statement such as, "I like the way you tried using the steps of self-control!"
   - If students use the steps appropriately, reinforce them with a statement such as, "Great job using the steps of problem solving!"

4. If students fail to attempt the skill or perform it inappropriately, **model** it by acting out the steps. Next:

   - If students respond positively (attempt the skill steps), reinforce their attempts with a statement such as, "I like the way you tried to use the steps of accepting 'no'!" If students' attempts are successful, reinforce that with a statement such as, "Great job using the steps of self-control!"
   - If students attempt the skill but are unsuccessful, provide feedback and instruction on how to use the skill. A statement such as, "The next time Jeff teases you, you can stop, count to five, and think about your choices."
   - Prompt the student again to engage in the skill with a statement such as, "Try the steps of problem solving again."

5. If students fail to attempt the skill, or their attempts are still unsuccessful, provide **feedback** and **instruction** on how to use the skill with a statement such as, "When you lose a game, first stop and count to five. Then think about your choices and the consequences." Prompt students to use skills at a later date with a statement such as, "Why don't you try to use the steps of self-control later when you have the problem again?"

Skills Record presented in Figure 3-2 (Chapter 3) provides a useful format for establishing **two-way communication** between leaders and parents and teachers, and for obtaining weekly feedback about Tough Kids' utilization of social skills outside of the group.

Summary

In this chapter, a number of important considerations were raised about conducting social skills training sessions. These can be applied to any format that you choose: from small groups to classrooms to entire school programs. The main components of social skills training include discussion, modeling, role play, feedback, goal setting, and positive reinforcement. Other important group components include group rules, personal goals, homework, videotaping, booster sessions, and generalization procedures. Importantly, significant adults in Tough Kids' lives should use reinforcement, prompting, and modeling to liberally

assist students' use of their newly acquired skills in the real world.

Some of the information, or the components of the programs, might seem overwhelming. As a reminder, it will be helpful for you to try to work with another adult when setting up and conducting the groups. In the remaining chapters, outlines are presented that should help put all of the pieces together into a meaningful package. The lessons are presented in outline form to make it easy to use them in the group sessions. These include actual statements that leaders can use while conducting group sessions. Good luck, and remember to **have fun**!

CHAPTER 4

Reproducibles

Social Situations for Role Play

Student's Name: _____ Date: _____

Your Name: _____

This student is involved in a social skills group where he/she is learning how to improve his/her relationships with others. We would like your help in making the group a positive experience for this student. Please take a few minutes of your time and complete the following questions. We will use this information during the group as examples and situations for the student to work through. In this way, the things we do in group should be much more meaningful for him/her. Thank you!

Describe any general concerns you have about this student's friendships and social skills. In other words, generally speaking, how does this student get along with his/her peers?

Describe at least three specific problematic situations that recently occurred between this student and other students. Be specific with your examples.

1._____

_____

_____

_____

2._____

_____

_____

_____

3._____

_____

_____

_____

 Social Skills Contract

I agree to use my skills of _____,
(what?)

including all of the steps, this week. I will use the steps _____
(when?   how often?)

_____. I will keep track of my skills by

_____. If I meet this goal, I will earn
(how?)

_____.
(what?)

My Signature: _____

Parent's/Teacher's Signature: _____

Weekly Contract

I agree to use my skills of _____,
(what?)

including all of the steps, this week. I will use the steps _____
(when?   how often?)

_____. I will keep track of my skills by

_____. If I meet this goal, I will earn
(how?)

_____.
(what?)

My Signature: _____

Parent's/Teacher's Signature: _____

Homework Sheet

Name: _____

Date: _____

Skill to Practice

1.
2.
3.
4.
5.

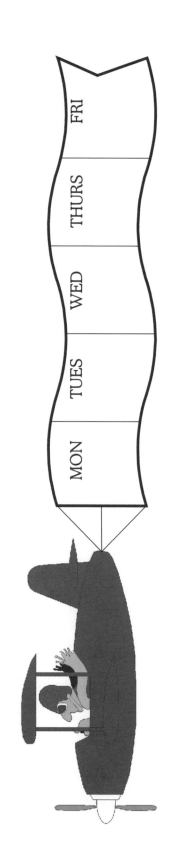

MON	TUES	WED	THURS	FRI

Part I—Social Skills Concepts

Weekly Homework Chart

Names

© 1995 by Sheridan, S.M. Available from Sopris West: Longmont, CO. (800) 547-6747

Part I—Social Skills Concepts

Social Skills
Homework Thermometer

HOT

and
getting . . .

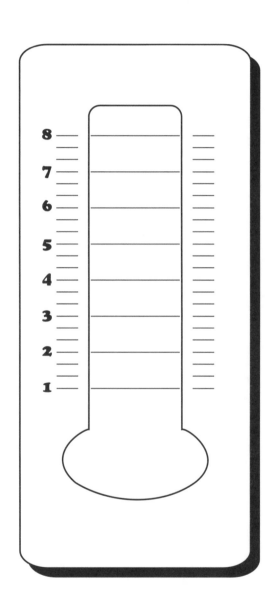

8
7
6
5
4
3
2
1

HOTTER!

has successfully
completed the
Friendship
Group!

Group Rules

1. Stay in your own space.
2. Participate.
3. Take turns speaking.
4. Speak in a nice voice.
5. Use nice words.

Part I—Social Skills Concepts

TRAINING

SESSION

OUTLINES

PART II

Introduction

In this section of the book, outlines for conducting social skills training sessions are presented. The outlines should be useful for conducting social skills training in small groups, classroom-based, or school-wide formats. Suggestions for increasing the effectiveness of each format are presented in How To Boxes II-1, II-2, and II-3 that follow the outlines. The outlines presented here are based on 60-minute sessions; however, the time can be altered to meet your own personal needs.

The primary components of the Tough Kid Social Skills Program are central to the structured outlines presented in this chapter. The forms, checklists, and other materials presented in Chapters 1-4 can be used in any combination to increase the usefulness of social skills training. Skill Sheets and Classroom Posters for each skill are also provided in this section.

Target Skills

There are at least three important components involved in students getting along with others.

> "The specific skills that you choose to include should be based on the particular needs of your students."

First, students must know how to start, or enter, a social situation or interaction appropriately. Second, they must know how to effectively keep the interaction going in a positive way. Third, students must know how to deal with problems or conflicts when they arise; better yet, how to behave in ways that allow them to avoid problems from occurring. These three skill areas—social entry, maintaining interactions, and solving problems—are often problematic for Tough Kids. Therefore, they are the focus of the social skills program.

Within the general areas of social entry, maintaining interactions, and solving problems, two or more specific subskills are taught during social skills training. The skills are taught in a step-by-step format to help Tough Kids retain the information. Box II-1 outlines the specific social skills and their steps.

It is not necessary to include all of the subskills listed in each outline in your social skills program. The specific skills that you choose to include should be based on the particular needs of your students. This will be determined using assessment procedures described in Chapter 2. The *Skills Survey* in Figure 2-3 (Chapter 2) can be especially helpful in narrowing in on the problem areas (subskills) that will be the focus of your social skills training sessions. Guidelines for Selecting Social Skills in How To Box 2-5 (Chapter 2) will help you to target particular social skills to focus on in training sessions.

Body Basics

As a rule, all of the skills taught in the program require the use of good body language. "Body Basics" should be reviewed toward the beginning of the group session, as they are an important and necessary component of the other skills.

Body basics are important nonverbal behaviors that should be an integral part of students' behaviors when engaging in social interactions. They include five behaviors that can be remembered by the acronym FEVER. The components of FEVER and their definitions are presented below:

1. **F**ace the other person (your body should be facing the other person, or your head should turn toward the other person when in a conversation).

2. Use **E**ye contact (your eyes should look at the face of the other person in a comfortable way; not on the floor, out the window, or staring inappropriately).

3. Use appropriate **V**oice (your voice should be clear and loud enough for the other person to hear, but not so loud that everyone around you can hear).

4. Use the right **E**xpression (your expression should match what you say and your tone of voice).

5. Use the right body posture—**R**elax (your hands, arms, and legs should be loose and relaxed; your fists should be relaxed and unclenched).

Skill Areas

The first set of skills taught is **Social Entry**. Specific behaviors (subskills) that are included in this area are: (1) starting conversations, (2) joining in, and (3) recognizing and expressing feelings. The second general skill area is **Maintaining Interactions**. Two specific subskills taught within this area include: (1) having a conversation, and (2) playing cooperatively. The third general skill is **Solving Problems**. Because Tough Kids seem to find themselves in many problem situations, solving problems is considered a **key skill** in the social skills program. When conducting social skills training, problem solving should be taught in such a way that the same steps can be used in a broad range of social situations. The specific behaviors targeted in the Tough Kids Social Skills Program include: (1) solving problems, (2) using self-control, (3) solving arguments, (4) dealing with teasing, (5) dealing with being left out, and (6) accepting "No." Clearly these are not the Tough Kids' only social problems. Once students learn the basic steps for solving problems and use them in these situations, they should be encouraged to apply these new skills to other problems and situations they face.

Opening Session

Introductions
(10 minutes)

If students are not familiar with you or with each other, begin the session with introductions. Consider making name tags or decorating folders as an initial activity.

A. **Group leaders**—Give your name (as you wish to be called in the social skills training sessions) and one thing about yourself to remember.

B. **Students**—Go around the group and have students provide:

1. Name.

2. Grade.

3. School (if different for all students).

4. One thing to remember about them or one thing they are good at.

Assessment
(15 minutes)

A. **Formal assessment**—At the leader's discretion, a formal assessment of Tough Kids' self-perceptions of their social skills may be desired. Standardized social skills scales such as those discussed in Chapter 2 (Box 2-1) can be used. Or, the *Skills Survey* (Figure 2-3) can be used as a simple instrument to assess students' ideas about their own abilities to perform the target skills.

B. **Informal assessment**—Behavioral observations are to be conducted informally throughout the first session.

Purpose of Group Sessions
(5 minutes)

There are at least two reasons for getting together/spending time each week talking about friendships and friendship skills. Inform students that the things the group will discuss and learn will help them to:

A. Learn how to make and keep friends.

B. Learn how to get along better with others.

Group Rules
(10 minutes)

A. **Lead a group discussion**—Generate four or five group rules and encourage students to be an active part of identifying the rules.

B. **Rules** should include:

1. Stay in your own space—Students are not allowed to engage in any physical contact, including hitting, shoving, or kicking.

2. Participate—Students are encouraged to involve themselves during discussions and role plays using personal examples and situations.

3. Take turns speaking—Interruptions and blurting out are not acceptable.

4. Speak in a nice voice—Yelling and loud voices are not appropriate for the group.

5. Use nice words—Name calling and aggressive statements are not allowed.

V
General Procedures
(10 minutes)

Each week the group will be learning some important things about getting along with others. Inform the students that the things the group will be doing will be similar from week to week. Each week the group will:

A. Learn about important **behaviors** to get along with others (obtain examples of behaviors that are of issue with group members).

B. Learn the **steps** to perform these important behaviors.

C. **Practice** the behaviors and watch others practice.

D. Provide others in the group with helpful **feedback** about how they performed the skill and behaved in the group.

E. Earn **snacks** if group rules are followed[*] (if rules are not followed or if behavior gets out of control, it is recommended that you implement a time out procedure in a corner and then in the hall).

F. Assign **homework**. Stickers will be earned and posted on a chart when homework is brought back completed.

G. Set **goals** and complete behavioral **contracts** with rewards and consequences. The goals will deal with practicing what is learned each week.

VI
Socialization Time
(10 minutes)

A. **Snacks** are provided to all if the students' behaviors were acceptable throughout the group session.

B. **Play time**—Observe students without adult contact (if possible) to allow for noninterrupted observations, and to informally assess students' social interactions.

*Snacks (e.g., granola bars, fruit rolls, or popcorn) are sometimes useful to keep students motivated to behave appropriately during social skills training sessions. In the group they are used as a short-term positive reinforcer to provide incentives to follow group rules and maintain behavioral control.

It is recommended that you use a **group vote** format to structure feedback that is provided to each student. First ask a student to report: (1) how he/she thinks he/she followed the rules that day, and (2) if he/she thinks he/she met his/her personal goal. Then, ask other students to provide specific feedback and vote on whether the student should earn a treat for the day (based on his/her behavior and attempts to work on his/her personal goal). Snacks are not seen as essential to the group, but the self-assessment and peer feedback are quite important.

Social Entry

Subskills of Social Entry

1. Body Basics/Starting a Conversation

2. Joining In

3. Recognizing and Expressing Feelings

Session 1

Subskill 1: Body Basics/ Starting a Conversation

Review From Previous Week
(3 minutes)

Promote retention of skills by posing the following questions:

A. What did we discuss last week?

B. Who can remember the group rules?

Introduce Body Basics
(7 minutes)

Introduce Body Basics in the following way:

A. One main reason for us being here is to help us learn how to make friends. There are two things that we will learn today: body basics and how to start conversations.

B. Body basics are actions that we should perform with others to let them know that we like them and that we are interested in them. It is important to learn the body basics well, because we will use them in everything we do with others.

C. What are the body basics? We can remember them by the word FEVER. (Show steps of FEVER listed on poster [see Classroom Posters section]. Display the poster in a prominent place throughout the ten-week group. Demonstrate each body basic as it is presented.)

1. **F**ace the other person.

2. Use **E**ye contact.

3. Use appropriate **V**oice

4. Use the right **E**xpression.

5. Use the right body posture—**R**elax.

D. There are certain things you need to remember to do and not do when using body basics. (Time permitting, have students generate as many **dos** and **don'ts** as possible; write responses on the board. If time does not allow for a discussion, try to incorporate these points into the general discussion.)

Dos and Don'ts for Body Basics

Do:
- Stay in your own space.
- Count to five or ten if you need to help yourself relax.
- Smile.

Don't:
- Stare at the other person.
- Get too close or be too far away.
- Use clenched fists or jaw.
- Stick out tongue or use other inappropriate gestures.

Introduce Starting a Conversation
(10 minutes)

Introduce Starting a Conversation in the following way:

A. We are going to practice the body basics at the same time we learn to start conversations with friends.

1. Starting a conversation is one important way to make friends. When you see someone that you like or someone that you would like to play with or talk to, it is important to know how to appropriately start a conversation with him/her.

2. When you are learning something new, such as how to do a math problem or ride a bike, you often learn important steps or rules. Just like steps or rules for math, there are steps for how to start a conversation with friends.

3. There are right ways and wrong ways to start conversations with other kids. If you know and follow the steps, you can do it the right way. (Emphasize that students can have control over their social behaviors.)

B. **Steps for Starting a Conversation** (display classroom poster).

1. Body basics (FEVER).

2. Greet the other person (use the person's name and say "Hi," "How are you?" etc.).

3. Decide what to say (practice in your mind if necessary).

4. Wait for the appropriate time (do not interrupt).

5. Start speaking (use an appropriate tone of voice).

C. **Describe each step**, including the information in parentheses. Elicit examples of each step from group.

D. Inform students that there are certain things they need to remember to do and not do when starting a conversation. Time permitting, have students generate as many **dos** and **don'ts** as possible; write responses on the board. If time does not allow for a discussion, try to incorporate these points into the general discussion.

Dos and Don'ts of Starting a Conversation

Do:
- Remember the body basics (repeat as necessary).
- Smile.
- Use nice words.

Don't:
- Yell or whisper unless necessary.
- Interrupt the other person if he/she is working or talking.
- Use inappropriate words.
- Get too close to the other person.

E. **Model** the skill with one leader demonstrating how to start a conversation with a co-leader or student volunteer. Use **think aloud** procedures by vocalizing the steps as they are being demonstrated. Time permitting, demonstrate both appropriate and inappropriate uses of the skill.

F. Assess and discuss demonstration. Have students identify the steps that were demonstrated. Include an assessment of the body basics that were used.

Student Role Plays
(20 minutes)

A. Select two volunteers to conduct a role play in front of the group. Use student-generated scenarios to the greatest extent possible. Have group members provide feedback. Continue until each student attempts to role play **starting a conversation**.

B. Use scenarios below as needed (appropriate actions follow in parentheses):

1. You want to walk home from school with a boy who lives in your neighborhood. What are you going to do? (Ask him if he would like to walk home together.)

2. Your mom said you could have a friend over to play on Saturday. You want Tim to come over. What are you going to do? (Ask him if he would like to come over.)

3. The teacher said that you could work on an assignment with one other student. You want to ask Lisa. What are you going to do? (Ask her to work together.)

4. You saw a good movie over the weekend. You want to tell Sam about it. What are you going to do? (Start a conversation about the movie.)

5. There is a new boy in school. You want to sit with him at lunch. What are you going to do? (Ask him to eat lunch together.)

Introduction to and Instructions for Homework Sheets and Weekly Contracts
(5 minutes)

A. Each week, the group will be setting goals and using *Homework Sheets* to enable students to practice new skills at home and school. Demonstrate goal setting and self-monitoring on the forms. Examples to present to students follow:

1. Your homework this week is to start conversations with friends as much as possible. You are going to set a goal (something you will work toward) for starting conversations. On your *Weekly Contract* (see Figure 4-2, Chapter 4), write down how many times you think you start conversations the right way. Then, set a goal by writing down how many times you think you can start a conversation using body basics and the steps you have learned in your social skills group. We will be talking about what you can earn if you meet your goal.

2. On the other side of the *Weekly Contract* is your *Homework Sheet* (see Figure 4-3, Chapter 4 or Skill Sheets at the back of this book). There are boxes on this side of the form with the days of the week listed. In the boxes, you will put a checkmark (or "X" or sticker) each time you start a conversation with a friend. Make one mark for each conversation you start. This will help you keep track of how you are doing meeting your goal.

B. It is important that students bring in their *Weekly Contract* and *Homework Sheets* each week in order to discuss how their weeks went. When they bring their sheets back with everything filled in, students are allowed to select a sticker to put on the *Class Homework Chart*. (Remember that other reinforcement systems can be used, such as Mystery Motivators or Spinners. See suggestions in Chapter 4.)

VI

Group Discussion/Performance Feedback/Vote for Snack
(5 minutes)

A. Go through the group and discuss each student:*

 1. How did _____ follow the rules today? Did he/she . . . ?

 2. How did _____ do on his/her personal goal?

 3. Besides the rules, what was one thing that _____ did that you liked? (Use I-statements, such as "I thought it was good when you remembered to use eye contact when starting a conversation.") What could _____ have done better?

*You may want to begin by asking each student about his/her own behavior before requesting feedback from other students.

B. Leaders also need to provide positive feedback for each student.

C. Provide snacks for those who earned them.

VII

Goal Setting and Behavior Contract
(10 minutes)

A. Establish a behavior contract with each student by completing the *Weekly Contract*. The two leaders should circulate among students to help complete and check their contracts. It may also be preferable to hold off writing the contract, and allow the students and their classroom teachers or parents to be responsible for their completion.

B. Each student's behavioral goal for the week should be related to **body basics/starting a conversation**.

C. Ensure that details of the program are complete, including a specific goal, identification of what will be earned, and when and how it will be earned.

D. Encourage each student to use the *Homework Sheet* to keep track of (self-monitor) their behaviors.

Session 2

Subskill 2: Joining In

I

Review From Previous Week
(5 minutes)

A. Collect *Homework Sheets* and provide reinforcers for students who brought them back.

B. Discuss contracts and deliver reinforcers to those who met goal (if appropriate).

II

Introduce Joining In
(15 minutes)

Introduce Joining In in the following way:

A. Last week we discussed body basics and starting a conversation. We said that they are important to use in order to make friends. You all practiced starting a conversation in group, home, and at school. This week we are going to learn another way to make friends. You can make friends by asking other kids if you can **join them** in a game or activity.

B. What does it mean to **join in**? (Have students generate as many responses as possible, and offer the following examples.)

 1. To play with others who are already playing a game.

 2. To do something with a group of other kids.

C. Why is it important to know how to join in? (Have students generate as many responses as possible, and offer the following examples.)

1. To be able to play with others.

2. To have fun with a group of kids.

3. To become part of a group.

D. Just like there were steps for starting a conversation, there are steps or rules for joining in. There are right ways and wrong ways to join in. It is important to know these steps so that you can join in with other kids in a **friendly** and **appropriate** way. (Emphasize that students have control over their social behaviors.)

E. **Steps for Joining In** (display classroom poster).

1. Body basics (FEVER).

2. Greet the other person (use the person's name and say "Hi," "How are you?" etc.).

3. Wait for the right time (do not interrupt and make sure they are paying attention).

4. Ask to join (ask using a nice voice).

F. **Describe each step**, including the information in parentheses. Elicit examples of each step from students.

G. Inform students that there are certain things they need to remember to do and not do when joining in. Time permitting, have students generate as many **dos** and **don'ts** as possible; write responses on the board. If time does not allow for a discussion, try to incorporate these points into the general discussion.

Dos and Don'ts of Joining In

Do: • Remember the body basics (repeat as necessary).
 • Smile.
 • Use nice words.

Don't: • Yell or whisper.
 • Interrupt the other person if he/she is working or talking.
 • Use inappropriate words.
 • Get uncomfortably close to the other person.

H. **Model** the skill with one leader demonstrating joining in with a co-leader or group volunteer. Use **think aloud** procedures by vocalizing the steps as they are being demonstrated. Time permitting, demonstrate both appropriate and inappropriate uses of the skill.

I. Assess and discuss demonstration. Have students identify the steps that were demonstrated. Include an assessment of the body basics that were used.

III
Student Role Plays
(25 minutes)

A. Select two volunteers to conduct a role play in front of the group. Use student-generated scenarios to the greatest extent possible. Have group members provide feedback. Continue until each student attempts to role play **joining in**.

B. Use scenarios below as needed (appropriate actions follow in parentheses):

1. You are at school and you see some kids playing basketball on the playground. You want to play. What are you going to do? (Ask one of the kids if you can join in.)

2. Some kids are playing video games before school. You would like to play. What are you going to do? (Ask if you can play too.)

3. Two kids are sitting together at lunch. You want to eat lunch with them. What are you going to do? (Ask if you can eat lunch with them.)

4. Your teacher said that you could work on a social studies project with two other kids. Peter and Enrique are already working together and you want to be part of their group. What are you going to do? (Ask them if you can join their group.)

5. Kelly and Ali are planning on going to the mall on Saturday. You would like to go with them. What are you going to do? (Ask if you can join them on Saturday.)

Group Discussion/Performance Feedback/Vote for Snack
(5 minutes)

A. Go through the group and discuss each student:*

1. How did _____ follow the rules today? Did he/she . . . ?

2. How did _____ do on his/her personal goal?

3. Besides the rules, what was one thing that _____ did that you liked? (Use I-statements.) What could _____ have done better?

*You may want to begin by asking each student about his/her own behavior before requesting feedback from other students.

B. Leaders also need to provide positive and constructive feedback for each student.

C. Provide snacks for those who earned them.

V

Goal Setting and Behavior Contract
(10 minutes)

A. Establish behavior contracts with students by completing the backs of the *Homework Sheets*. The two leaders should circulate among students to help complete and check their contracts. It may also be preferable to hold off writing the contracts, and allow students and their classroom teachers or parents to be responsible for their completion.

B. Each student's behavioral goal for the week should be related to **joining in**.

C. Ensure that details of the program are complete, including a specific goal, identification of what will be earned, and when and how it will be earned.

D. Encourage each student to use the *Homework Sheet* to keep track of (self-monitor) their behaviors.

Session 3

Subskill 3: Recognizing and Expressing Feelings

Review from Previous Week
(5 minutes)

A. Collect *Homework Sheets* and provide reinforcers for students who brought them back.

B. Discuss contracts and deliver reinforcers to those who met goal (if appropriate).

Introduce Recognizing and Expressing Feelings
(15 minutes)

Introduce Recognizing and Expressing Feelings in the following way:

A. One thing that is important in making friends is noticing how others feel, and saying how you feel. Why is it important to notice how you feel or how others feel?

1. It can help us understand ourselves and the other person.

2. To show the other person that we care about him/her.

3. So that others know how we feel.

4. To let others understand our feelings and change their behavior toward us.

5. So our feelings do not get stored up inside and cause us to hurt inside.

6. So our feelings do not come out in a way that we do not want. (Explain that stored up feelings can cause us to lose control.)

B. Ask the group, "What are some feelings that you sometimes have?" (Have students generate a list of feeling words and write them on the board. Remind students that "angry" or "mad" are usually secondary feelings that are usually preceded by other feelings. Discuss what these first feelings might be.)

C. Ask students the following: "How can you tell how you feel?" "How can you tell how others feel?" Provide these examples:

1. Body cues such as clenched fists or jaw, upset stomach, glaring eyes, slumped or still posture.

2. Facial cues such as smiles, frowns, or tears.

3. Voice tone such as whispering or yelling.

D. Inform students that just as there are steps involved in effectively starting a conversation and joining in, there are also steps for recognizing and expressing feelings.

E. **Steps for Recognizing and Expressing Feelings** (display classroom poster).

1. Body basics (FEVER).

2. Decide how you feel/how the other person feels.

3. Wait for a good time.

4. Think about your choices and their consequences.

   • Say how you feel starting with, "I feel . . . ."
   • Ask the other person if he/she feels that way.
   • Ask if you can help.

5. Act out your best choice.

F. **Describe each step**. Elicit examples of each step from students.

G. **Model** the skill with one leader demonstrating recognizing and expressing feelings with a co-leader or group volunteer. Use **think aloud** procedures by vocalizing the steps as they are being demonstrated. Time permitting, demonstrate both appropriate and inappropriate uses of the skill.

H. Assess and discuss demonstration. Have students identify the steps that were demonstrated. Include an assessment of the body basics that were used.

Student Role Plays
(25 minutes)

A. Select two volunteers to conduct a role play in front of the group. Use student-generated scenarios to the greatest extent possible. Have group members provide feedback. Continue until each student attempts to role play **recognizing and expressing feelings**.

B. Use scenarios below as needed:

1. One of the boys in your class is having a birthday party. Most of the other boys are invited, but you are not. How do you feel? What will you do?

2. You are playing video games with your brother. He beats you at your favorite game every time. How do you feel? What will you do?

3. You are playing football with some other students at school. Even though you are wide open, no one ever throws the ball to you. How do you feel? What will you do?

4. Your mom tells you that you cannot go to the mall with your brother. You really want to go. How do you feel? What will you do?

5. You are on the playground at school and a bully calls you a "wimp." How do you feel? What will you do?

6. There is a new student at school who is sitting alone at lunch. All the other kids walk by her laughing and having fun. How does she feel? What will you do?

7. Your friend's dog was hit by a car yesterday, and now they have to put it to sleep. Your friend really loved her dog. How does your friend feel? What will you do?

8. You studied hard for a spelling test but only got half of the words right. The boy who sits next to you starts to laugh when he sees your paper. How do you feel? What will you do?

Group Discussion/Performance Feedback/Vote for Snack
(5 minutes)

A. Go through the group and discuss each student:*

1. How did _____ follow the rules today? Did he/she . . . ?

2. How did _____ do on his/her personal goal?

3. Besides the rules, what was one thing that _____ did that you liked? (Use I-statements.) What could _____ have done better?

*You may want to begin by asking each student about this/her own behavior before requesting feedback from other students.

B. Leaders also need to provide positive and constructive feedback for each student.

C. Provide snacks for those who earned them.

Goal Setting and Behavior Contract
(10 minutes)

A. Establish behavior contracts with students by completing the backs of the *Homework Sheets*. The two leaders should circulate among students to help complete and check their contracts. It may also be preferable to hold off writing the contracts, and allow students and their classroom teachers or parents to be responsible for their completion.

B. Each student's behavioral goal for the week should be related to **recognizing and expressing feelings**.

C. Ensure that details of the program are complete, including a specific goal, identification of what will be earned, and when and how it will be earned.

D. Encourage each student to use the *Homework Sheet* to keep track of (self-monitor) their behaviors.

Skill Area B

Maintaining Interactions

Subskills of Maintaining Interactions

4. Having a Conversation

5. Playing Cooperatively

Session 4

Subskill 4: Having a Conversation

Review from Previous Week
(5 minutes)

A. Collect *Homework Sheets* and provide reinforcers for students who brought them back.

B. Discuss contracts and deliver reinforcers to those who met goal (if appropriate).

Introduce Having a Conversation
(15 minutes)

Introduce Having a Conversation in the following way:

A. So far, we have discussed body basics, starting a conversation, and joining in. We said that they were all important when making friends. You all practiced them here and in other places. Today we are going to learn what to do once you start a conversation or join in. After you start a conversation, you have to **keep it going**. This is an important way to make great friends.

B. What is a conversation? (Have students generate as many responses as possible, and offer the following examples.)

1. A way of spending time with another person by speaking about something.

2. Speaking about school, movies, sports, something you both like or that you have in common, etc.

C. Why is it important to know how to have a conversation? (Have students generate as many responses as possible, and offer the following examples.)

1. To be able to talk to others.

2. To tell others something important.

3. To find out something from others.

D. Just as there were steps for starting a conversation, there are also steps or rules for keeping one going. There are right ways and wrong ways for keeping a conversation going. It is important to know these steps so that you can have a conversation with other students in a friendly and appropriate manner. (Emphasize that students have control over their social behaviors.)

E. **Steps for Having a Conversation** (display classroom poster).

1. Body basics (FEVER).

2. Wait your turn (do not interrupt others or monopolize the conversation).

3. Say what you want to say (be clear and straightforward).

4. Listen to the other person (pay attention).

5. Say at least two more things to the other person (keep the conversation going by asking two more questions or making two more comments).

6. Make a closing remark ("Goodbye," "See you later.")

F. **Describe each step**, including the information in parentheses. Elicit examples of each step from students.

G. Inform students that there are certain things they need to remember to do and not do when keeping a conversation going. Time permitting, have students generate as many **dos** and **don'ts** as possible; write responses on the board. If time does not allow for a discussion, try to incorporate these points into the general discussion.

Dos and Don'ts of Having a Conversation

Do:	• Remember the body basics (repeat as necessary).
	• Smile.
	• Use nice words.

Don't:	• Yell or whisper unless necessary.
	• Interrupt the other person if he/she is working or talking.
	• Use inappropriate words.

H. **Model** the skill with one leader demonstrating how to have a conversation with a co-leader or group volunteer. Use **think aloud** procedures by vocalizing the steps as they are being demonstrated. Time permitting, demonstrate both appropriate and inappropriate uses of the skill.

I. Assess and discuss demonstration. Have students identify the steps that were demonstrated. Include an assessment of the body basics that were used.

III
Student Role Plays
(25 minutes)

A. Select two volunteers to conduct a role play in front of the group. Use student-generated scenarios to the greatest extent possible. Have group members provide positive and negative feedback. Continue until each student attempts to role play **having a conversation**.

B. Use scenarios below as needed.

1. You want to walk home from school with a boy who lives in your neighborhood. Ask him if he would like to walk home with you. Keep the conversation going.

2. You are at school and see some kids playing "Go Fish." You want to play. Ask one of the kids if you can join in. Keep the conversation going.

3. You are excited about a football game you saw on TV over the weekend. You want to talk to your friend about it. Go up to your friend, start a conversation, and keep it going.

4. The teacher said that you could work on a project with one other student. You want to ask Penny. Ask her to work together. Keep a conversation going about the project.

5. Your favorite TV show was on last night. It is also Jamal's favorite show. You want to talk to him about it. Start a conversation and keep it going.

Group Discussion/Performance Feedback/Vote for Snack
(5 minutes)

A. Go through the group and discuss each student:*

1. How did _____ follow the rules today? Did he/she . . . ?

2. How did _____ do on his/her personal goal?

3. Besides the rules, what was one thing that _____ did that you liked? (Use I-statements.) What could _____ have done better?

*You may want to begin by asking each student about his/her own behavior before requesting feedback from other students.

B. Leaders also need to provide positive and constructive feedback for each student.

C. Provide snacks for those who earned them.

V
Goal Setting and Behavior Contract
(10 minutes)

A. Establish behavior contracts with the students by completing the backs of the *Homework Sheets*. The two leaders should circulate among students to help complete and check their contracts. It may also be preferable to hold off writing the contracts, and allow students and their classroom teachers or parents to be responsible for their completion.

B. Each student's behavioral goal for the week should be related to **having a conversation**.

C. Ensure that details of the program are complete, including a specific goal, identification of what will be earned, and when and how it will be earned.

D. Encourage each student to use the *Homework Sheet* to keep track of (self-monitor) their behaviors.

Session 5
Subskill 5: Playing Cooperatively

Review from Previous Week
(5 minutes)

A. Collect *Homework Sheets* and provide reinforcers for students who brought them back.

B. Discuss contracts and deliver reinforcers to those who met goal (if appropriate).

Introduce Playing Cooperatively
(15 minutes)

Introduce Playing Cooperatively in the following way:

A. In the last few weeks we have discussed body basics, starting a conversation, joining in, and having a conversation. We said that they were important in order to make and keep friends. You all practiced having a conversation in group, at home, and at school. This week we are going to learn another skill that is important to keep friends: **playing cooperatively**. Once you start a conversation and keep it going, you will often want to play with the other person. This is an important way to make great friends.

B. What does it mean to **cooperate**? (Elicit as many examples as possible from group members and offer the following examples.)

1. To play together in a fair way.

2. To share, take turns, and help each other.

C. Why is it important to know how to play co-operatively? (Elicit as many examples as possible from group members and offer the following examples.)

1. So everyone knows what to do.

2. To be able to get along when playing.

3. To make the game more fun.

D. Inform students that just as there are steps for starting and having a conversation, there are also steps or rules for **playing coopera-tively**. There are right ways and wrong ways for playing a game, and it is important to know these steps so that everyone can play together in a friendly and appropriate man-ner. (Emphasize that students have control over their social behaviors.)

E. **Steps for Playing Cooperatively** (display classroom poster).

1. Body basics (FEVER).

2. Decide who starts (flip a coin, roll a die).

3. Wait your turn (do not go out of turn).

4. Speak and listen to the other person (have a conversation).

5. Say something nice at the end ("Good game," "That was fun," "Thanks for playing." Discuss with students how to handle losing if necessary).

F. **Describe each step**, including the informa-tion in parentheses. Elicit examples of each step from students.

G. Inform students that there are certain things they need to remember to do and not do when playing with other students. Time permit-ting, have students generate as many **dos** and **don'ts** as possible; write responses on the board. If time does not allow for a discus-sion, try to incorporate these points into the general discussion.

Dos and Don'ts of Playing Cooperatively

Do:
- Remember the body basics (repeat as necessary).
- Smile.
- Use nice words.
- Look at the directions if you do not know them.

Don't:
- Yell or whisper unless necessary.
- Interrupt the other person if he/she is speaking.
- Use inappropriate words.
- Argue about the rules or game.
- Be a sore loser.

H. **Model** the skill with one leader demonstrat-ing playing cooperatively with a co-leader or group volunteer. Use **think aloud** proce-dures by vocalizing the steps as they are be-ing demonstrated. Time permitting, demonstrate both appropriate and inappro-priate uses of the skill.

I. Assess and discuss demonstration. Have stu-dents identify the steps that were demon-strated. Include an assessment of the body basics that were used.

III
Student Role Plays
(25 minutes)

A. Select two volunteers to conduct a role play in front of the group. Use student-generated sce-narios to the greatest extent possible. Instruct students to start a conversation, and follow with playing cooperatively. Have group members provide positive and constructive feedback. Continue until each student at-tempts to role play **playing cooperatively**.

B. Use scenarios below as needed:

1. You see two other kids playing "Rock, Scissors, Paper." You would like to play along. Ask if you can join in; play

cooperatively for a few minutes; have a conversation while playing.

2. You are at school and see some kids playing "Old Maid." You want to play along. Ask one of the students if you can join in; play cooperatively for a few minutes; keep a conversation going while playing.

3. You want to play a game with a new student in your class. Ask her to play; play cooperatively for a few minutes; keep a conversation going while you play.

4. The teacher said that you could play with one other person quietly for the last ten minutes of school. Ask one student to play a game; play cooperatively and keep a conversation going while you play.

5. You want to organize a game of touch football during recess. Ask a few kids to play; play cooperatively for a few minutes.

IV

Group Discussion/Performance Feedback/Vote for Snack
(5 minutes)

A. Go through the group and discuss each student:*

1. How did _____ follow the rules today? Did he/she . . . ?

2. How did _____ do on his/her personal goal?

3. Besides the rules, what was one thing that _____ did that you liked? (Use I-statements.) What could _____ have done better?

*You may want to begin by asking each student about his/her own behavior before requesting feedback from other students.

B. Leaders also need to provide positive and constructive feedback for each student.

C. Provide snacks for those who earned them.

V

Goal Setting and Behavior Contract
(10 minutes)

A. Establish behavior contracts with students by completing the backs of the *Homework Sheets*. The two leaders should circulate among students to help complete and check their contracts. It may also be preferable to hold off writing the contracts, and allow students and their classroom teachers or parents to be responsible for their completion.

B. Each student's behavioral goal for the week should be related to **playing cooperatively**.

C. Ensure that details of the program are complete, including a specific goal, identification of what will be earned, and when and how it will be earned.

D. Encourage students to use the *Homework Sheet* to keep track of (self-monitor) their behaviors.

Problem Solving

Subskills of Problem Solving

6. Solving Problems

7. Using Self-Control

8. Solving Arguments

9. Dealing With Teasing

10. Dealing With Being Left Out

11. Accepting "No"

Session 6
Subskill 6: Solving Problems

Review From Previous Week
(5 minutes)

A. Collect *Homework Sheets* and provide reinforcers for students who brought them back.

B. Discuss contracts and deliver reinforcers to those who met goal (if appropriate).

Introduce Solving Problems
(15 minutes)

Introduce Solving Problems in the following way:

A. One main reason for us to be in this group is because even though we like to play with our friends, we sometimes have problems. We need to learn how to solve our problems with our friends, parents, and brothers and sisters.

B. What are some problems that you sometimes have with friends? (Generate a list of three to five student responses.)

1. Arguing about what game to play.

2. Fighting about rules of a game.

3. Disagreeing about an answer during school.

C. Just as there are steps or rules for starting a conversation, playing cooperatively, etc., there are also steps for solving problems. If you know and follow the rules, you can solve your problems with friends in a friendly and appropriate manner, just like you can solve other problems. (Emphasize that students have control over their social behaviors.)

D. **Steps for Solving Problems** (display classroom poster).

1. Stop, take a deep breath, and count to five. (Identify this step as particularly

important to help relax, use self-control, and begin thinking about choices. Have students practice this step if necessary. This is important to help students relax and start thinking about what the problem is that they have to face.)

2. Decide what the problem is and how you feel. (Provide examples of problems and have students identify what the problem is. Help students to identify feelings by using I-statements ["I feel sad when others tease me"]. When students identify "mad" or "angry" as feelings, discuss these as secondary feelings that are usually preceded by other feelings [e.g., sad, upset, embarrassed, disappointed]. Inform students that if they are with someone else, they should tell that person what they think the problem is. They might feel mad, but there is always a feeling that comes first. Try to think about those other feelings.)

3. Think about your choices and their consequences. (Have students identify at least three choices. Discuss **consequences** as things that happen as a result of an action. Following each choice, identify possible consequences. Prompt students to think about what they can do to solve the problem. It is very important to think about what might happen as a result of each choice. Suggest that they present a choice to the other person to solve the problem.)

4. Decide on your best choice. (Have the group decide on the best choice for the discussed problem by consensus. This can be accomplished by voting, discussion, etc. Prompt students to think about what might happen, and select the choice that they think is best and has the best consequences.)

5. Do it. (This step requires students to engage in the choice that was agreed upon. Remind students to use body basics

while completing this step. Following this step, discuss with students the importance of asking themselves, "How did I do?")

E. **Describe each step**, including the information in parentheses.

F. Inform students that there are certain things they need to remember to do and not do when solving problems. Time permitting, have students generate as many **dos** and **don'ts** as possible; write responses on the board. If time does not allow for a discussion, try to incorporate these points into the general discussion.

Dos and Don'ts for Solving Problems

Do:
- Relax.
- Tell yourself to calm down.
- Think of at least three choices.

Don't:
- Yell or scream.
- Call the other person names.
- Hit or kick the other person.

G. **Model** the skill with one leader demonstrating solving problems with a co-leader or group volunteer. Use **think aloud** procedures by vocalizing the steps as they are being demonstrated. Time permitting, demonstrate both appropriate and inappropriate uses of the skill.

H. Assess and discuss demonstration. Have students identify the steps that were demonstrated. Include an assessment of the body basics that were used.

III
Student Role Plays
(25 minutes)

A. Select two volunteers to conduct a role play in front of the group. Use student-generated scenarios to the greatest extent possible. Instruct students to use the problem-solving steps in order to deal with the situation. Have group members provide feedback. Continue until each student attempts to role play **solving problems**.

B. Use scenarios below as needed:

1. You are walking home from school and you realize that you forgot your spelling list. You have a spelling test the next day, and your mom told you that if you forget your spelling list one more time, you will not get your allowance. What is the problem? What are your choices? Act out your best choice.

2. Marty is a big troublemaker at your school. He calls kids names, acts like a bully, and picks fights. He just called you a "stupid jerk and baby" for no reason. Your mom promised to take you to the amusement park if you stayed out of fights. What is the problem? What are your choices? Act out your best choice.

3. You want to walk home from school with Maria, a girl who lives in your neighborhood. You finally get the courage to ask Maria to walk home with you, but she says no because she is going to Patty's house after school. You really wanted to walk home with Maria, and besides, she always goes to Patty's house. What is the problem? What are your choices? Act out your best choice.

4. You are invited to Stan's birthday party at a pizza parlor on Saturday. You want to go, but your parents told you that you must go to your cousin's wedding instead. Stan is your best friend, and you really want to go to the party. What is the problem? What are your choices? Act out your best choice.

5. Although your little brother is not allowed in your room, he went in and took your portable video game to show his friends. One of his friends grabbed it and dropped it, and now it does not work anymore. Your brother is very sad and said that he was sorry. What is the problem? What are your choices? Act out your best choice.

IV

Group Discussion/Performance Feedback/Vote for Snack
(5 minutes)

A. Go through the group and discuss each student:*

1. How did _____ follow the rules today? Did he/she . . . ?

2. How did _____ do on his/her personal goal?

3. Besides the rules, what was one thing that _____ did that you liked? (Use I-statements.) What could _____ have done better?

*You may want to begin by asking each student about his/her own behavior before requesting feedback from other students.

B. Leaders also need to provide positive and constructive feedback for each student.

C. Provide snacks for those who earned them.

V

Goal Setting and Behavior Contract
(10 minutes)

A. Establish behavior contracts with students by completing the backs of the *Homework Sheets*. The two leaders should circulate among students to help complete and check their contracts. It may also be preferable to hold off on writing the contracts, and allow students and their classroom teachers or parents to be responsible for their completion.

B. Each student's behavioral goal for the week should be related to **solving problems**.

C. Ensure that details of the program are complete, including a specific goal, identification of what will be earned, and when and how it will be earned.

D. Encourage each student to use the *Homework Sheet* to keep track of (self-monitor) their behaviors.

Session 7
Subskill 7: Using Self-Control

Review From Previous Week
(5 minutes)

A. Collect *Homework Sheets* and provide reinforcers for students who brought them back.

B. Discuss contracts and deliver reinforcers to those who met goal (if appropriate).

Introduce Using Self-Control
(15 minutes)

Introduce Using Self-Control in the following way:

A. We have talked a lot about solving problems. The steps we learned are important because they can help us to use **self-control** when we are faced with a problem. What are some times that you lose control? (Generate as many situations from students as possible, and offer the following examples.)

1. When we get angry, disappointed, or frustrated.

2. When we do not get our way.

3. When we fight, argue, or yell at someone.

B. What happens when you lose self-control? (Generate as many ideas from students as possible. Identify the following examples as consequences of losing self-control.)

1. We get into trouble with our parents or teachers.

2. We do not get along with other kids; we lose friends.

3. We do not feel good about ourselves.

C. Why is it important to use self-control? (Generate as many ideas from students as possible and offer the following examples.)

1. To get along with others.

2. To feel better about ourselves.

3. To solve problems calmly and keep friends.

D. Just as there are steps for solving problems and other skills, there are also steps for using self-control. The steps for using self-control are the same as for solving problems. If you know and follow the rules, you can use self-control with friends in a friendly and appropriate manner, just like you can solve other problems. (Emphasize that students have control over their social behaviors.)

E. **Steps for Using Self-Control** (display classroom poster).

1. Stop, take a deep breath, and count to five.

2. Decide what the problem is and how you feel.

3. Think about your choices and their consequences (identify the following as possible choices):

- Ignore the situation.
- Tell yourself "It's OK."
- Tell yourself to relax.
- Speak calmly.
- Compromise.
- Say how you feel, using I-statements.

4. Decide on your best choice.

5. Do it.

F. **Discuss** the steps of using self-control, using a specific example from a student.

   1. What is the problem?

   2. What are your choices? (Generate a list and write on board.)

   3. What might happen if you choose _____? (Identify these as consequences; write them on the board.)

   4. What is the best thing to do?

   5. Act out your best choice, using body basics.

G. Inform students that there are certain things they need to remember to do and not do when using self-control. Time permitting, have students generate as many **dos** and **don'ts** as possible; write responses on the board. If time does not allow for a discussion, try to incorporate these points into the general discussion.

Dos and Don'ts for Using Self-Control

Do:
- Relax.
- Tell yourself to calm down.
- Think of at least three choices that may solve the problem.

Don't:
- Yell or scream.
- Call the other person names.
- Hit or kick the other person.

H. **Model** the skill with one leader demonstrating using self-control with a co-leader or group volunteer. Use **think aloud** procedures by vocalizing the steps as they are being demonstrated. Time permitting, demonstrate both appropriate and inappropriate uses of the skill.

I. Assess and discuss demonstration of specific problem solving/self-control steps. Include an assessment of the body basics that were used.

III
Student Role Plays
(25 minutes)

A. Select two volunteers to conduct a role play in front of the group. Use student-generated scenarios if possible. Instruct students to use problem solving/using self-control steps. Have group members provide feedback. Continue until each student attempts to role play **using self-control**.

B. Use scenarios below as needed:

   1. You and your friend, Eli, are sitting around deciding what to do one day. Eli wants to play catch, but you want to play video games. What is the problem? What are your choices? Act out your best choice.

   2. You are playing video games and your mom tells you to set the table for dinner. You do not want to but your mom said that if you do not, you will not be able to play video games for the rest of the day. What is the problem? What are your choices? Act out your best choice.

   3. You are coloring at the kitchen table. Your brother accidentally bumps your arm, your hand slips, and you have a big mark on your paper. What is the problem? What are your choices? Act out your best choice.

   4. You and a group of friends are playing soccer. Your team is losing by one point. Just as you are about to try to score a goal, your teammate accidentally runs into you and knocks you over. You fall and cannot kick the goal. What is the problem? What are your choices? Act out your best choice.

   5. You are watching your favorite TV show when your brother walks into the room. He wants to watch a different TV show and starts to argue with you. What is the

problem? What are your choices? Act out your best choice.

6. Another student at school calls you a "no brain dummy" because you go to the resource room for part of the day. He gets some other kids to laugh at you with him. What is the problem? What are your choices? Act out your best choice.

7. It is your sister's birthday and your parents are taking her to a pizza parlor and a movie. You want to go, but there are not enough tickets. What is the problem? What are your choices? Act out your best choice.

IV

Group Discussion/Performance Feedback/Vote for Snack
(5 minutes)

A. Go through the group and discuss each student:*

1. How did _____ follow the rules today? Did he/she . . . ?

2. How did _____ do on his/her personal goal?

3. Besides the rules, what was one thing that _____ did that you liked? (Use I-statements.) What could _____ have done better?

*You may want to begin by asking each student about his/her own behavior before requesting feedback from other students.

B. Leaders also need to provide positive and constructive feedback for each student.

C. Provide snacks for those who earned them.

V

Goal Setting and Behavior Contract
(10 minutes)

A. Establish behavior contracts with students by completing the backs of the *Homework*

Sheets. The two leaders should circulate among students to help complete and check their contracts. It may also be preferable to hold off writing the contracts, and allow students and their classroom teachers or parents to be responsible for their completion.

B. Each student's behavioral goal for the week should be related to **using self-control**.

C. Ensure that details of the program are complete, including a specific goal, identification of what will be earned, and when and how it will be earned.

D. Encourage each student to use the *Homework Sheet* to keep track of (self-monitor) their behaviors.

Session 8

Subskill 8: Solving Arguments

Review From Previous Week
(5 minutes)

A. Collect *Homework Sheets* and provide reinforcers for students who brought them back.

B. Discuss contracts and deliver reinforcers to those who met goal (if appropriate).

Introduce Solving Arguments
(15 minutes)

Introduce Solving Arguments in the following way:

A. One main reason for us to be in this group is because even though we like to play with our friends, we sometimes have problems. One common problem we have with friends is getting into arguments. How many of you get into arguments with friends or brothers or sisters?

B. What are some things you might argue about with your friends? (Generate a list of three to five problems from students, and offer the following examples.)

    1. The right answer on an assignment.

    2. What television show or movie to watch.

    3. The rules of a game.

C. Inform the students that just as there are steps for starting a conversation, playing coopera-tively, solving problems, etc., there are steps or rules for solving arguments. The steps for solving arguments are the same as for solv-ing problems. If you know and follow the steps, you can use self-control and solve your arguments in a friendly and appropriate manner. (Emphasize that students have con-trol over their social behaviors.)

D. **Steps for Solving Arguments** (display classroom poster).

    1. Stop, take a deep breath, and count to five.

    2. Decide what the problem is and how you feel.

    3. Think about your choices and their con-sequences (identify the following as pos-sible choices):

        *   Compromise.
        *   Take turns.
        *   Ask someone else.
        *   Speak calmly.
        *   Tell yourself, "It's OK."
        *   Say how you feel in a friendly way.

    4. Decide on your best choice.

    5. Do it.

E. **Discuss** with students the process of problem solving when solving arguments, using a specific example from a student.

    1. What is the problem? (An argument.)

2. What are your choices? (Generate a list and write on board.)

3. What might happen if you choose _____? (Identify these as consequences, write them on the board.)

4. What is the best thing to do?

5. Act out your best choice, using body basics.

F. Inform students that there are certain things they need to remember to do and not do when solving arguments. Time permitting, have students generate as many **dos** and **don'ts** as possible; write responses on the board. If time does not allow for a discussion, try to incorpo-rate these points into the general discussion.

Dos and Don'ts for Solving Arguments

Do:
*   Relax.
*   Tell yourself to calm down.
*   Think of at least three choices that may solve the problem.
*   Compromise.

Don't:
*   Yell or scream.
*   Call the other person names.
*   Argue back.

H. **Model** the skill with one leader demonstrat-ing solving arguments with a co-leader or group volunteer. Use **think aloud** proce-dures by vocalizing the steps as they are be-ing demonstrated. Time permitting, demonstrate both appropriate and inappro-priate uses of the skill.

I. Assess and discuss demonstration of specific problem-solving steps as they were used to solve the argument. Include an assessment of the body basics that were used.

III
Student Role Plays
(25 minutes)

A. Select two volunteers to conduct a role play in front of the group. Use student-generated scenarios if possible. Instruct students to use problem-solving steps to solve the argument. Have group members provide feedback. Continue until each student attempts to role play **how to solve arguments**.

B. Use scenarios below as needed:

1. You are at home on a Saturday afternoon with your friend from school. Your younger brother comes into the room where you're playing and wants to hang out with the two of you. You tell your brother to get out but he keeps saying "You can't make me!" and arguing that it's his house too. What is the problem? What are your choices? Act out your best choice.

2. You stayed after school one day, and your teacher asked you to help clean up the classroom after a messy art project. Your teacher left the room for a minute, and another student, Jake, came in as you were standing over his desk. Jake yelled, "You're snooping in my desk and taking my things!" Even though you were not snooping, he argues that you are always looking through his things and probably even stealing them. What is the problem? What are your choices? Act out your best choice.

3. You are playing checkers with a friend, Tammy, at her house. Tammy has to get up to answer the telephone. When she returns to the game, she thinks that you moved one of the pieces, but you did not. You try to tell her that you did not cheat, and an argument begins. What is the problem? What are your choices? Act out your best choice.

4. You call your mom from school because you forgot to bring your permission slip for an upcoming field trip. You ask your mom to bring it in because this is the last day that you can turn it in. Your mom refuses to bring it in because she's on her way to work and besides, she reminded you all week to bring it and you ignored her. You begin to argue with her because you really need the permission slip. What is the problem? What are your choices? Act out your best choice.

5. Your dad has two tickets to a basketball game and promised to take you if you finish your homework before dinner. You really want to go, but you watched TV after school and didn't finish your math and spelling assignments. After dinner your dad is getting ready for the game and decides to bring your younger brother since his homework was completed. You argue with him because he said you could go. What is the problem? What are your choices? Act out your best choice.

IV
Group Discussion/Performance Feedback/Vote for Snack
(5 minutes)

A. Go through the group and discuss each student:*

1. How did _____ follow the rules today? Did he/she . . . ?

2. How did _____ do on his/her personal goal?

3. Besides the rules, what was one thing that _____ did that you liked? (Use I-statements.) What could _____ have done better?

*You may want to begin by asking each student about his/her own behavior before requesting feedback from other students.

B. Leaders also need to provide positive and constructive feedback for each student.

C. Provide snacks for those who earned them.

V

Goal Setting and Behavior Contract
(10 minutes)

A. Establish behavior contracts with students by completing the backs of the *Homework Sheets*. The two leaders should circulate among students to help complete and check their contracts. It may also be preferable to hold off writing the contracts, and allow students and their classroom teachers or parents to be responsible for their completion.

B. Each student's behavioral goal for the week should be related to **solving arguments**.

C. Ensure that details of the program are complete, including a specific goal, identification of what will be earned, and when and how it will be earned.

D. Encourage students to use the *Homework Sheet* to keep track of (self-monitor) their behaviors.

Session 9

Subskill 9: Dealing With Teasing

I

Review From Previous Week
(5 minutes)

A. Collect *Homework Sheets* and provide reinforcers for students who brought them back.

B. Discuss contracts and deliver reinforcers to those who met goal (if appropriate).

II

Introduce Dealing With Teasing
(15 minutes)

Introduce Dealing With Teasing in the following way:

A. We have talked about a lot of problems that we have with friends. One problem that many of us have is when other students tease us. Who knows what teasing means? (Generate as many responses from students as possible, and offer the following examples.)

1. When other students make fun of something you say or do.

2. When other kids say mean things about you.

3. When someone gives you a hard time because of how you look, or because you are different than them.

B. Why do some students tease other kids? (Have students generate as many reasons as possible. This discussion is important for students to begin understanding others' perspectives. It also helps students see that by reacting to the teasing, they are giving the other person what he/she wants: a reaction. Offer the following examples in addition to student responses).

1. They are trying to get attention.

2. They think they are cool.

3. They do not like themselves very much.

4. They might be jealous of something good about you.

5. They are trying to "push your buttons" and get a reaction.

C. Just as there are steps for starting a conversation, playing cooperatively, using self-control, etc., there are steps for dealing with teasing. There are right ways and wrong ways to deal with teasing. If you know and follow the steps, you can deal with teasing in a friendly and appropriate manner, just like you can solve other problems. The steps will be easy to remember, because they are the same steps that we learned for solving problems and arguments. And it's important that you use self-control when dealing with teasing. (Emphasize that students have control over their social behaviors.)

D. **Steps for Dealing With Teasing** (display classroom poster).

1. Stop, take a deep breath, and count to five.

2. Decide what the problem is and how you feel.

3. Think about your choices and their consequences (identify the following as possible choices):

   • Ignore the teasing.
   • Walk away.
   • Say something good about yourself to yourself or the other person.
   • Say how you feel in a friendly way.

4. Decide on your best choice.

5. Do it.

E. Have students provide examples of teasing. Discuss the process of problem solving when dealing with teasing.

1. What is the problem? (Being teased.)

2. What are your choices? (Generate a list and write it on the board.)

3. What might happen if you choose _____? (Identify these as consequences, write them on the board.)

4. What is the best thing to do?

5. Act out the best choice, using body basics.

F. Inform students that there are certain things they need to remember to do and not do when dealing with teasing. Time permitting, have

students generate as many **dos** and **don'ts** as possible; write responses on the board. If time does not allow for a discussion, try to incorporate these points into the general discussion.

Dos and Don'ts for Dealing With Teasing

Do: • Relax.
     • Tell yourself to calm down.
     • Tell yourself, "It's OK."

Don't: • Yell or scream.
        • Call the other person names.
        • Give comebacks.

G. **Model** the skill with one leader demonstrating dealing with teasing with a co-leader or group volunteer. Use **think aloud** procedures by vocalizing the steps as they are being demonstrated. Time permitting, demonstrate both appropriate and inappropriate uses of the skill.

H. Assess and discuss demonstration of specific steps. Have group members provide feedback. Include an assessment of the body basics that were used.

III

Student Role Plays
(25 minutes)

A. Select two volunteers to conduct a role play in front of the group. Use student-generated scenarios to the greatest extent possible. Have group members provide feedback. Continue until each student attempts to role play **dealing with teasing**.

B. Use scenarios below as needed:

1. You see some students playing jump rope on the playground and you want to play along. You walk over to them and ask if you can join. They laugh at you and say that you are "too clutzy" to play. What is the problem? How do you feel?

What are your choices? Act out your best choice.

2. You got a new haircut for a family picture that is going to be taken soon. Lots of your buddies begin teasing you, saying your new "buzz" is dorky. Your teacher won't let you wear your baseball cap in the classroom, and your friends keep rubbing your head laughing at your haircut. What is the problem? How do you feel? What are your choices? Act out your best choice.

3. You call Patrice on the phone and ask her if she can play on Saturday. She says that she has plans with someone else, and they do not want you to play with them. What is the problem? How do you feel? What are your choices? Act out your best choice.

4. You are playing with your dolls and your brother comes into the room. He starts making fun of you for "playing with such baby toys." What is the problem? How do you feel? What are your choices? Act out your best choice.

5. You are at the park playing tennis with a friend. Some other kids are watching you play, and they start making fun of how you swing the tennis racket. You hate it when kids tease you. What is the problem? How do you feel? What are your choices? Act out your best choice.

IV

Group Discussion/Performance Feedback/Vote for Snack
(5 minutes)

A. Go through the group and discuss each student:*

1. How did _____ follow the rules today? Did he/she . . . ?

2. How did _____ do on his/her personal goal?

3. Besides the rules, what was one thing that _____ did that you liked? (Use I-statements.) What could _____ have done better?

*You may want to begin by asking each student about his/her own behavior before requesting feedback from other students.

B. Leaders also need to provide positive and constructive feedback for each student.

C. Provide snacks to those who earned them.

Goal Setting and Behavior Contract
(10 minutes)

A. Establish behavior contracts with students by completing the backs of the *Homework Sheets*. The two leaders should circulate among students to help complete and check their contracts. It may also be preferable to hold off writing the contracts, and allow the students and their classroom teachers or parents to be responsible for their completion.

B. Each student's behavioral goal for the week should be related to **dealing with teasing**.

C. Ensure that details of the program are complete, including a specific goal, identification of what will be earned, and when and how it will be earned.

D. Encourage students to use the *Homework Sheet* to keep track of (self-monitor) their behaviors.

Session 10

Subskill 10: Dealing With Being Left Out

Review from Previous Week
(5 minutes)

A. Collect *Homework Sheets* and provide reinforcers for students who brought them back.

B. Discuss contracts and deliver reinforcers to those who met their goal (if appropriate).

Introduce Dealing With Being Left Out
(15 minutes)

Introduce Dealing With Being Left Out in the following way:

A. We have talked about a lot of problems that we have with friends. One problem that many of us have is that we are sometimes left out of things. What does it mean to be **left out**? (Have students generate as many responses as possible, and offer the following examples.)

 1. When other students leave us out of games, activities, etc.

 2. When everyone else is doing something and we are not included.

B. Why do some students leave others out? (Have students generate as many reasons as possible. This discussion is important for students to begin to understand others' perspectives. It also helps students see that by reacting to others, they are giving the other person what he/she wants: a reaction. Offer the following examples in addition to student responses.)

 1. They might not realize that you have been left out.

 2. They might not know that you want to play.

 3. They might not know how you feel.

 4. They think they are cool.

 5. They do not like themselves very much.

 6. They might be jealous of something good about you.

C. In our group we have learned how to solve problems, use self-control, and how to deal with teasing. Dealing with being left out is a lot like dealing with teasing. In fact, the steps for dealing with being left out will be easy to remember, because they are the same steps that we learned for solving problems and dealing with teasing. And like other problems, it's important to use self-control to solve the problem. (Emphasize that students have control over their social behaviors.)

D. **Steps for Dealing With Being Left Out** (display classroom poster).

 1. Stop, take a deep breath, and count to five.

 2. Decide what the problem is and how you feel.

 3. Think about your choices and their consequences (identify the following as possible choices):

 • Ask to join in.
 • Say how you feel using I-statements.
 • Play with someone else.
 • Do something else that is fun.

 4. Decide on the best choice.

 5. Do it.

E. Inform students that there are certain things they need to remember to do and not do when dealing with being left out. Time permitting, have students generate as many **dos** and **don'ts** as possible; write responses on the board. If time does not allow for a discussion, try to incorporate these points into the general discussion.

Dos and Don'ts for Dealing With Being Left Out

Do:
- Relax.
- Use body basics.
- Think good thoughts about yourself.

Don't:
- Pout.
- Call the other person names.
- Interrupt other people.

F. **Model** the skill with one leader demonstrating how to deal with being left out with a co-leader or group volunteer. Use **think aloud** procedures by vocalizing the steps as they are being demonstrated. Time permitting, demonstrate both appropriate and inappropriate uses of the skill.

G. Assess and discuss demonstration of specific steps for dealing with being left out. Include an assessment of the body basics that were used.

Student Role Plays
(25 minutes)

A. Select two volunteers to conduct a role play in front of the group. Use student-generated scenarios if possible. Instruct students to use problem-solving steps to deal with being left out. Have group members provide feedback. Continue until each student attempts to role play **how to deal with being left out**.

B. Use scenarios below as needed:

1. You are playing alone on the playground and see some kids playing basketball. You want to play along. What is the problem? How do you feel? What are your choices? Act out your best choice.

2. Your brother is playing with a friend from school. You want to play with them, but they say only two people can play this game. How do you feel? What is the problem? What are your choices? Act out your best choice.

3. Stephanie is having a sleep-over birthday party this weekend. You find out from Jenny that lots of kids are going. You were not invited. What is the problem? How do you feel? What are your choices? Act out your best choice.

4. Some kids at school are picking sides for a kickball game. Neither of the captains picks you. How do you feel? What is the problem? What are your choices? Act out your best choice.

5. Many of the girls in your class are eating lunch at the same table in the lunchroom. You are sitting alone. What is the problem? How do you feel? What are your choices? Act out your best choice.

6. You are finishing your math assignment during recess because you did not get it done earlier. The other students are all playing a game on the playground. You want to play. What is the problem? How do you feel? What are your choices? Act out your best choice.

7. You tried out for the soccer team but did not make it. Most of your friends made the team and have practice every night after school and a game every Saturday. You're not part of the team. What is the problem? What are your choices? Act out your best choice.

IV
Group Discussion/Performance Feedback/Vote for Snack
(5 minutes)

A. Go through the group and discuss each student:*

   1. How did _____ follow the rules to-day? Did he/she . . . ?

   2. How did _____ do on his/her personal goal?

   3. Besides the rules, what was one thing that _____ did that you liked? (Use I-statements.) What could _____ have done better?

*You may want to begin by asking each student about his/her own behavior before requesting feedback from other students.

B. Leaders also need to provide positive and constructive feedback for each student.

C. Provide snacks for those who earned them.

V
Goal Setting and Behavior Contract
(10 minutes)

A. Establish behavior contracts with students by completing the backs of the *Homework Sheets*. The two leaders should circulate among students to help complete and check contracts. It may also be preferable to hold off writing the contracts, and allow students and their classroom teachers or parents to be responsible for their completion.

B. Each student's behavioral goal for the week should be related to **dealing with being left out**.

C. Ensure that details of the program are complete, including a specific goal, identification of what will be earned, and when and how it will be earned.

D. Encourage students to use the *Homework Sheet* to keep track of (self-monitor) their behaviors.

Session 11
Subskill 11: Accepting "No"

I
Review From Previous Week
(5 minutes)

A. Collect *Homework Sheets* and provide reinforcers for students who brought them back.

B. Discuss contracts and deliver reinforcers to those who met their goal (if appropriate).

II
Introduce Accepting "No"
(15 minutes)

Introduce Accepting "No" to students in the following way:

A. We have talked about a lot of problems that we have with friends. One problem that many of us have is when we want to do something, but we are told that we cannot do it. In other words, we are told "No." This can happen with friends, parents, or brothers and sisters. What are some situations where you have been told "No"? (Have group members generate as many examples as possible, and offer the following examples.)

   1. Wanting to spend the night at a friend's house.

   2. Asking for extra money or candy.

   3. Inviting a friend to play.

   4. Asking a teacher for a special privilege.

B. Why are we sometimes told "No"? (Have group members provide as many reasons as possible, and offer the following examples.)

1. Parents or teachers want us to do something else.

2. Friends have other plans.

3. Others do not have time.

4. Because parents and teachers are in charge.

C. In our group we have learned the steps involved in solving problems and how to use those same steps with other problems, such as dealing with teasing and being left out. In addition, being told "No" is another problem for which you can use problem-solving steps. (Emphasize that students have control over their social behaviors.)

D. **Steps for Accepting "No"** (display classroom poster).

1. Stop, take a deep breath, and count to five.

2. Decide what the problem is and how you feel.

3. Think about your choices and their consequences (identify the following as possible choices):

   • Say "OK." (accept the answer)
   • Say how you feel in a friendly way.
   • Find something else to do.

4. Decide on your best choice.

5. Do it.

E. **Discuss** each step. Generate choices from students and write them on the board. Discuss the potential consequences for each choice and vote on best choices.

F. Inform students that there are certain things they need to remember to do and not do when accepting "No." Time permitting, have students generate as many **dos** and **don'ts** as possible; write responses on the board. If time

does not allow for a discussion, try to incorporate these points into the general discussion.

Dos and Don'ts for Accepting "No"	
Do:	• Relax. • Tell yourself to calm down. • Tell yourself, "It's OK."
Don't:	• Talk back. • Pout or whine. • Yell back.

G. **Model** the skill with one leader demonstrating how to accept "No" with a co-leader or group volunteer. Use **think aloud** procedures by vocalizing the steps as they are being demonstrated. Time permitting, demonstrate both appropriate and inappropriate uses of the skill.

H. Assess and discuss demonstration of specific problem-solving steps when accepting "No." Have group members provide feedback. Include an assessment of the body basics that were used.

III

Student Role Plays
(25 minutes)

A. Select two volunteers to conduct a role play in front of the group. Use student-generated scenarios to the greatest extent possible. Have group members provide feedback. Continue until each student attempts to role play **accepting "No."**

B. Use scenarios below as needed:

1. You are playing alone on the playground and decide that you want to play catch. You want to play with another girl who is standing alone. You ask her to play, but she says "No" and runs away. What is the problem? How do you feel? What are your choices? Act out your best choice.

2. Your teacher is allowing some students to go to the library to work on a group project. You want to be part of that group. You ask her if you can go but she says "No." What is the problem? How do you feel? What are your choices? Act out your best choice.

3. You want to ask a friend over to spend the night. It is a school night, and your mom says "No." What is the problem? How do you feel? What are your choices? Act out your best choice.

4. Your dad tells you that you cannot go to the basketball game with your brother. You really want to go. What is the problem? How do you feel? What are your choices? Act out your best choice.

5. Your sister is having a birthday party. You ask her if you can come. She says "No." What is the problem? How do you feel? What are your choices? Act out your best choice.

6. You are watching some kids play chess at school. You want to play next, but someone else is already waiting. You ask to play, and they say "No." What is the problem? How do you feel? What are your choices? Act out your best choice.

7. Your parents have some friends over and are planning to go out to dinner. You want to go too, but they say "No." What is the problem? How do you feel? What are your choices? Act out your best choice.

IV

Group Discussion/Performance Feedback/Vote for Snack
(5 minutes)

A. Go through the group and discuss each student:*

1. How did _____ follow the rules today? Did he/she . . . ?

2. How did _____ do on his/her personal goal?

3. Besides the rules, what was one thing that _____ did that you liked? (Use I-statements.) What could _____ have done better?

*You may want to begin by asking each student about his/her own behavior before requesting feedback from other students.

B. Leaders also need to provide positive and constructive feedback for each student.

C. Provide snacks for those who earned them.

V

Goal Setting and Behavior Contract
(10 minutes)

A. Establish behavior contracts with students by completing the backs of the *Homework Sheets*. The two leaders should circulate among students to help complete and check their contracts. It may also be preferable to hold off writing the contracts, and allow students and their classroom teachers or parents to be responsible for their completion.

B. Each student's behavioral goal for the week should be related to **accepting "No."**

C. Ensure that details of the program are complete, including a specific goal, identification of what will be earned, and when and how it will be earned.

D. Encourage each student to use the *Homework Sheet* to keep track of (self-monitor) their behaviors.

Last Session

Review From Previous Week
(5 minutes)

A. Collect *Homework Sheets* and provide reinforcers for students who brought them back.

B. Discuss contracts and deliver reinforcers to those who met their goal (if appropriate).

Review Group Lessons
(20 minutes)

A. Exhibit classroom posters on the board and discuss each skill separately.

   1. Review social skill steps.

   2. Select one student to role play each social skill.

B. Distribute scrapbooks with skills identified.

C. Have each student identify at least one thing they learned in the group.

Post-Treatment Assessment
(10 minutes)

A. **Formal assessment**—At the leader's discretion, a formal assessment of Tough Kids' self-perceptions of their social skills may be desired. Standardized social skills scales such as those presented in Chapter 2 (Box 2-1) can be used. Or, the *Skills Survey* (Figure 2-3) can be used as a simple instrument to assess students' ideas about their own abilities to perform the target skills. If a pretreatment assessment was conducted in the Introductory Session, the same instrument should be used here.

B. **Informal assessment**—Behavioral observations are to be conducted informally throughout the last session.

Party
(25 minutes)

A. Distribute plain t-shirts and fabric markers.

B. Discuss procedures for decorating t-shirts.

   1. Encourage students to draw or display something on their t-shirts to help them remember the group experience (e.g., the problem-solving steps, body basics, etc.).

   2. Display a completed shirt.

C. Allow students to make t-shirts while eating or during another special treat.

D. Have students and leaders sign autograph pages in scrapbooks.

E. Distribute certificate of completion (see Figure 4-7, Chapter 4).

Booster Session

General Review
(5 minutes)

A. Welcome and Reintroductions.

B. Review group rules and procedures (e.g., discussion, practice, vote, snack).

C. Review personal goals.

Reintroduce Topic of Solving Problems
(15 minutes)

Reintroduce the topic to students in the following way:

A. One main reason that we began this group was to help us learn how to solve our problems with our friends, parents, and brothers and sisters.

B. What are some problems that you have had with friends since our last group? (Generate list of three to five problems from students).

C. You probably remember that we talked about rules for solving problems with friends. We spent a lot of time going over and practicing the rules here and at home, so you know that you are capable of solving problems you have with your friends. (Emphasize that students have control over their social behaviors.)

D. **Steps for Solving Problems** (display classroom poster).

1. Stop, take a deep breath, and count to five.

2. Decide what the problem is.

3. Think about your choices and their consequences.

4. Decide on your best choice.

5. Do it.

E. Select an example from the list of problems previously generated by students; discuss the steps of solving problems as they relate to the specific problem.

1. What is the problem?

2. What are your choices? (Generate list and write it on the board.)

3. What might happen if you choose ___? (Identify these as consequences; write them on the board.)

4. What is the best thing to do? (Consider a group vote.)

F. **Model** the skill with one leader demonstrating problem-solving steps with a co-leader or group volunteer. Use **think aloud** procedures by vocalizing the steps as they are being demonstrated. Time permitting, demonstrate both appropriate and inappropriate uses of the skill.

Student Role Plays
(25 minutes)

A. Select two volunteers to conduct a role play in front of the group. Use student-generated scenarios if possible. Have group members provide feedback. Continue until each student attempts to role play **problem-solving procedures**.

B. Use scenarios below as needed:

1. You want to walk home from school with Maria, a girl who lives in your neighborhood. You finally get the courage to ask Maria to walk home with you, but she says no because she is going to Patty's house after school. What is the problem? What are your choices? Act out your best choice.

2. You and your friend Carl are sitting around deciding what to do one day. Carl wants to play catch, but you want to play video games. What is the problem? What are your choices? Act out your best choice.

3. You stayed after school one day, and your teacher asked you to help clean up the classroom after a messy art project. Your teacher left the room for a minute, and another student, Jake, came in as you were standing over his desk. Jake yelled, "You're snooping in my desk and taking my things!" What is the problem? What are your choices? Act out your best choice.

4. Marty is a big troublemaker at your school. He calls kids names, acts like a bully, and picks fights. He just called you a "stupid jerk and baby" for no reason. Your mom promised to take you to the amusement park if you stayed out of fights. What is the problem? What are your choices? Act out your best choice.

5. You are playing checkers with a friend, Tammy, at her house. Tammy has to get up to answer the telephone. When she returns to the game, she thinks that you moved one of the pieces, but you did not. What is the problem? What are your choices? Act out your best choice.

6. You are walking home from school and you realize that you forgot your spelling list. You have a spelling test the next day, and your mom told you that if you forget your spelling list one more time, you will not get your allowance. What is the problem? What are your choices? Act out your best choice.

7. You and a group of friends are playing soccer. Your team is losing by one point. Just as you are about to try to score a goal, your teammate accidentally runs into you and knocks you over. You fall and cannot kick the goal. Your team loses the game. What is the problem?

What are your choices? Act out your best choice.

IV

Group Discussion/Performance Feedback/Vote for Snack
(5 minutes)

A. Go through the group and discuss each student:*

   1. How did _____ follow the rules today? Did he/she . . . ?

   2. How did _____ do on his/her personal goal?

   3. Besides the rules, what was one thing that _____ did that you liked? (Use I-statements.) What could ___ have done better?

*You may want to begin by asking each student about his/her own behavior before requesting feedback from other students.

B. Leaders also need to provide positive feedback for each student.

C. Provide snacks for those who earned them.

V

Goal Setting and Behavior Contract
(10 minutes)

A. Establish behavior contracts with students by completing the backs of the *Homework Sheets*. The two leaders should circulate among students to help complete and check their contracts. It may also be preferable to hold off writing the contracts, and allow the students and their classroom teachers or parents to be responsible for their completion.

B. Each student's behavioral goal should be related to **solving problems**.

C. Ensure that details of the program are complete, including a specific goal, identification of what will be earned, and when and how it will be earned.

D. Encourage each student to use the *Homework Sheet* to keep track of (self-monitor) their behaviors.

How To Box II-1

Increasing the Effectiveness of Small Group Social Skills Training

1. Identify a group of four to eight students with similar social concerns, using teacher references, behavioral checklists and rating scales, sociometrics, direct observational procedures, and other methods outlined in Chapter 2.

2. Obtain parental consent for involving students in the social skills group.

3. Collect information from parents and teachers regarding general and specific concerns they have about students' social skills and behaviors. Use this information to select the skills to target in the group training. The *Skills Survey* (see Figure 2-3, Chapter 2) and procedures in How To Box 2-5 might be useful.

4. Meet with parents and teachers for an informational meeting. Discuss the objectives of social skills training, ways they can help meet those objectives, and the need for open communication and collaboration to increase the effectiveness of the training. Also, describe for them all of the group procedures, including what will take place in the social skills training groups, when they will be conducted, how long they will last, students' homework, and the possibility of

parental involvement in delivering home reinforcers for good social skills and behaviors.

5. Establish a positive reinforcement system to promote skill usage inside and outside of the group. Decide on the general procedures (e.g., contracts, homework, tokens, or self-monitoring), and the mechanism for delivering reinforcers (e.g., Spinners, Mystery Motivators, or charts). See Chapter 4 for details.

6. Remain in close contact with teachers and parents to continually collect information about Tough Kids' social concerns, as well as parental perception of the effectiveness of social skills training. Consider using the *Weekly Social Skills Record* to keep track of training effectiveness (see Figure 3-2, Chapter 3).

7. Conduct an evaluation of the social skills program using checklists, rating scales, sociometrics, and direct observations. Ideally, direct observations should be conducted continually throughout the intervention. The measures used should be the same ones used in Step 3 to allow for direct comparisons.

How To Box II-2

Increasing the Effectiveness of Classroom-Based Social Skills Training

1. Work with a classroom teacher to identify the need and desirability of conducting classroom-based social skills training. Express the importance of sharing the responsibilities for conducting training and encouraging skill usage outside of training sessions.

2. Check into school policy for obtaining parental consent for the classroom social skills intervention.

3. Collect information from parents and teachers regarding general and specific concerns they have about students' social skills and behaviors. Use this information to select the skills to target in the classroom training. The *Skills Survey* form (see Figure 2-3, Chapter 2) and procedures in How To Box 2-5 will be useful in targeting.

4. Recruit assistance from the classroom teacher and other support staff. Ideally, persons who could be involved include school psychologists, school counselors, social workers, office staff, special educators, parents, and volunteers. At the very least, such persons should be informed of the program and requested to help reinforce the use of skills outside of the classroom.

5. Set up a reinforcement program that includes individual programs or group-based contingencies. Contracts, token systems, and self-monitoring are also useful for classroom-based procedures (see Chapter 4).

6. Promote skill usage outside of the classroom with homework and self-monitoring. Verbal cues (prompts) and demonstration of skills that can be applied to real life situations are also useful.

7. Meet with parents or communicate the objectives of the classroom-based training in writing. Request parents' assistance in meeting the objectives of the program. This can be accomplished through soliciting their help as volunteers and setting up Home-School Note programs (where parents deliver reinforcers at home in response to their child's positive social behaviors at school).

8. Conduct an evaluation of the social skills program using checklists, rating scales, sociometrics, and direct observations. Ideally, direct observations should be conducted continually throughout the intervention. The measures used should be the same ones used in Step 3 to allow for direct comparisons.

How To Box II-3

Increasing the Effectiveness of School-Wide Social Skills Training

1. Work with school administrators, classroom teachers, and others (staff and parents) to identify the need and desirability of conducting a school-wide social skills training program. Express the importance of sharing the responsibility for conducting training sessions and encouraging students' skill usage in all school settings.

2. Check into school policy for obtaining parental consent for the school-based social skills intervention.

3. Collect information from parents and teachers regarding general and specific concerns they have about students' social skills and behaviors. Use this information to select the skills to target in the school-wide training. The *Skills Survey* (see Figure 2-3, Chapter 2) and procedures in How To Box 2-5 will be useful in targeting.

4. Solicit support and assistance from all school staff, including administrators, teachers, certified personnel, parents, and other staff (e.g., office, lunchroom, playground, and custodial staff).

5. Conduct staff training for all individuals who will be involved in social skills training (ideally, this will be **everyone**). Carefully review the overall objectives and specific procedures and mechanics of the school-wide program, including classroom training sessions, ways for encouraging skill usage in all school settings, reinforcement systems, roles and responsibilities, etc.

6. If you have the help of other school staff, consider supplementing the school-wide program with small group training for the **really Tough Kids**. Procedures similar to the ones for conducting small groups (How To Box II-1) can be used to solicit and train those students who need more intensive social skills training.

7. Set up a school-wide reinforcement system that includes individual, classroom-based, or other programs to increase students' skill usage outside of the formal social skills training sessions. See Chapter 3 for suggestions, including How To Box 3-4.

8. Conduct weekly social skills sessions in classrooms using the outlines presented in this part of the book. Supplement the outlines with additional skill areas as needed. (A general session outline is presented in Box 4-1, Chapter 4.)

9. Conduct an evaluation of the social skills program using checklists, rating scales, sociometrics, and direct observations. Ideally, direct observations should be conducted continually throughout the intervention. The measures used should be the same ones used in Step 3 to allow for direct comparisons.

Box II-1

Steps of Target Social Skills

Starting a Conversation

1. Use Body basics.
2. Greet the other person.
3. Decide what to say.
4. Wait for the appropriate time.
5. Start speaking.

Joining In

1. Body basics.
2. Greet the other person.
3. Wait for the right time.
4. Ask to join.

Recognizing and Expressing Feelings

1. Body basics.
2. Decide how you feel/how the other person feels.
3. Wait for a good time.
4. Think about your choices and consequences:

    - Say how you feel, starting with "I feel . . . ."
    - Ask the other person if he/she feels that way.
    - Ask if you can help.

5. Act out your best choice.

Having a Conversation

1. Body basics.
2. Wait your turn.
3. Say what you want to say.

4. Listen to the other person.
5. Say at least two more things to the other person.
6. Make a closing remark.

Playing Cooperatively

1. Body basics.
2. Decide who starts.
3. Wait your turn.
4. Talk and listen to the other person.
5. Say something nice at the end.

Solving Problems

1. Stop, take a deep breath, and count to five.
2. Decide what the problem is and how you feel.
3. Think about your choices and their consequences.
4. Decide on your best choice.
5. Do it.

Using Self-Control

1. Stop, take a deep breath, and count to five.
2. Decide what the problem is and how you feel.
3. Think about your choices and their consequences:

    - Ignore the situation.
    - Tell yourself "It's OK."
    - Tell yourself to relax.
    - Speak calmly.
    - Say how you feel, using I-statements.

Box II-1 cont'd

4. Decide on your best choice.

5. Do it.

Solving Arguments

1. Stop, take a deep breath, and count to five.

2. Decide what the problem is and how you feel.

3. Think about your choices and their consequences:

   - Compromise.
   - Take turns.
   - Ask someone else.
   - Speak calmly.
   - Tell yourself "It's OK."
   - Say how you feel in a friendly way.

4. Decide on your best choice.

5. Do it.

Dealing With Teasing

1. Stop, take a deep breath, and count to five.

2. Decide what the problem is and how you feel.

3. Think about your choices and their consequences:

   - Ignore the teasing.
   - Walk away.
   - Say something good about yourself to yourself or to the other person.
   - Say how you feel in a friendly way.

4. Decide on your best choice.

5. Do it.

Dealing With Being Left Out

1. Stop, take a deep breath, and count to five.

2. Decide what the problem is and how you feel.

3. Think about your choices and their consequences:

   - Ask to join in.
   - Say how ~~~~ ing I-
   - Play w~~~~ ~~~~eone else.
   - Do something else that is fun.

4. Decide on your best choice.

5. Do it.

Accepting "No"

1. Stop, take a deep breath, and count to five.

2. Decide what the problem is and how you feel.

3. Think about your choices and their consequences:

   - Say "OK."
   - Say how you feel in a friendly way, using I-statements.
   - Find something else to do.

4. Decide on your best choice.

5. Do it.

Skill Sheets

Starting a Conversation

Name: _____ Date: _____

1. Body basics.
2. Greet the other person.
3. Decide what to say.
4. Wait for the appropriate time.
5. Start speaking.

These are all the times I used the skill this week:

MON	TUES	WED	THURS	FRI	SAT	SUN

Part II—Training Session Outlines

Joining In

Name: _____ Date: _____

1. Body basics.
2. Greet the other person.
3. Wait for the appropriate time.
4. Ask to join.

These are all the times I used the skill this week:

MON	TUES	WED	THURS	FRI	SAT	SUN

Recognizing and Expressing Feelings

Name: _____ Date: _____

1. Body basics.

2. Decide how you feel/how the other person feels.

3. Wait for a good time.

4. Think about your choices and their consequences:

    - Say how you feel, starting with "I feel . . . ."
    - Ask the other person if he/she feels that way.
    - Ask if you can help.

5. Act out your best choice.

These are all the times I used the skill this week:

MON	TUES	WED	THURS	FRI	SAT	SUN

Having a Conversation

Name: _____ Date: _____

1. Body basics.

2. Wait your turn.

3. Say what you want to say.

4. Listen to the other person.

5. Say at least two more things to the other person.

6. Make a closing remark.

These are all the times I used the skill this week:

MON	TUES	WED	THURS	FRI	SAT	SUN

Playing Cooperatively

Name: _____ Date: _____

1. Body basics.
2. Decide who starts.
3. Wait your turn.
4. Talk and listen to the other person.
5. Say something nice at the end.

These are all the times I used the skill this week:

MON	TUES	WED	THURS	FRI	SAT	SUN

Solving Problems

Name: _____ Date: _____

1. Stop, take a deep breath, and count to five.
2. Decide what the problem is and how you feel.
3. Think about your choices and their consequences.
4. Decide on your best choice.
5. Do it.

These are all the times I used the skill this week:

MON	TUES	WED	THURS	FRI	SAT	SUN

Using Self-Control

Name: _____ Date: _____

1. Stop, take a deep breath, and count to five.
2. Decide what the problem is and how you feel.
3. Think about your choices and their consequences:

   - Ignore the situation.
   - Tell yourself, "It's OK."
   - Tell yourself to relax.
   - Speak calmly.
   - Compromise.
   - Say how you feel, using I-statements.

4. Decide on your best choice.
5. Do it.

These are all the times I used the skill this week:

MON	TUES	WED	THURS	FRI	SAT	SUN

Solving Arguments

Name: _____ Date: _____

1. Stop, take a deep breath, and count to five.

2. Decide what the problem is and how you feel.

3. Think about your choices and their consequences:

   - Compromise.
   - Take turns.
   - Ask someone else.
   - Speak calmly.
   - Tell yourself, "It's OK."
   - Say how you feel in a friendly way.

4. Decide on your best choice.

5. Do it.

These are all the times I used the skill this week:

MON	TUES	WED	THURS	FRI	SAT	SUN

Part II—Training Session Outlines

Dealing With Teasing

Name: _____ Date: _____

1. Stop, take a deep breath, and count to five.
2. Decide what the problem is and how you feel.
3. Think about your choices and their consequences:
   - Ignore the teasing.
   - Walk away.
   - Say something good about yourself to yourself or the other person.
   - Say how you feel in a friendly way.
4. Decide on your best choice.
5. Do it.

These are all the times I used the skill this week:

MON	TUES	WED	THURS	FRI	SAT	SUN

Dealing With Being Left Out

Name: _____ Date: _____

1. Stop, take a deep breath, and count to five.
2. Decide what the problem is and how you feel.
3. Think about your choices and their consequences:
   - Ask to join in.
   - Say how you feel, using I-statements.
   - Play with someone else.
   - Do something else that is fun.
4. Decide on your best choice.
5. Do it.

These are all the times I used the skill this week:

MON	TUES	WED	THURS	FRI	SAT	SUN

Accepting "No"

Name: _____ Date: _____

1. Stop, take a deep breath, and count to five.
2. Decide what the problem is and how you feel.
3. Think about your choices and their consequences:
   - Say "OK."
   - Say how you feel in a friendly way, using I-statements.
   - Find something else to do.
4. Decide on your best choice.
5. Do it.

These are all the times I used the skill this week:

MON	TUES	WED	THURS	FRI	SAT	SUN

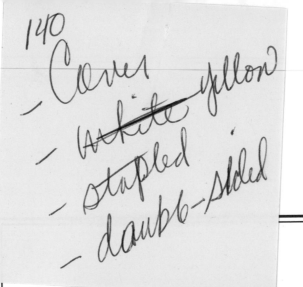

Classroom Posters

Body Basics

FEVER

1. **F**ace the other person.

2. Use **E**ye contact.

3. Use appropriate **V**oice.

4. Your **E**xpression should match what you say and your tone of voice.

5. Use the right body posture—**R**elax.

Starting a Conversation

1. Body basics.

2. Greet the other person.

3. Decide what to say.

4. Wait for the appropriate time.

5. Start speaking.

Part II—Training Session Outlines

Joining In

1. Body basics.

2. Greet the other person.

3. Wait for the appropriate time.

4. Ask to join.

Recognizing and Expressing Feelings

1. Body basics.

2. Decide how you feel/how the other person feels.

3. Wait for a good time.

4. Think about your choices and their consequences:

   - Say how you feel, starting with "I feel . . . ."

   - Ask the other person if he/she feels that way.

   - Ask if you can help.

5. Act out your best choice.

Having a Conversation

1. Body basics.

2. Wait your turn.

3. Say what you want to say.

4. Listen to the other person.

5. Say at least two more things to the other person.

6. Make a closing remark.

Playing Cooperatively

1. Body basics.

2. Decide who starts.

3. Wait your turn.

4. Talk and listen to the other person.

5. Say something nice at the end.

Solving Problems

1. Stop, take a deep breath, and count to five.

2. Decide what the problem is and how you feel.

3. Think about your choices and their consequences.

4. Decide on your best choice.

5. Do it.

Using Self-Control

1. Stop, take a deep breath, and count to five.

2. Decide what the problem is and how you feel.

3. Think about your choices and their consequences:

   - Ignore the situation.
   - Tell yourself, "It's OK."
   - Tell yourself to relax.
   - Speak calmly.
   - Compromise.
   - Say how you feel, using I-statements.

4. Decide on your best choice.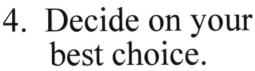

5. Do it.

Solving Arguments

1. Stop, take a deep breath, and count to five.

2. Decide what the problem is and how you feel.

3. Think about your choices and their consequences:

   - Compromise.
   - Take turns.
   - Ask someone else.
   - Speak calmly.
   - Tell yourself, "It's OK."
   - Say how you feel in a friendly way.

4. Decide on your best choice.

5. Do it.

Dealing With Teasing

1. Stop, take a deep breath, and count to five.

2. Decide what the problem is and how you feel.

3. Think about your choices and their consequences:

   - Ignore the teasing.
   - Walk away.
   - Say something good about yourself to yourself or the other person.
   - Say how you feel in a friendly way.

4. Decide on your best choice.

5. Do it.

Dealing With Being Left Out

1. Stop, take a deep breath, and count to five.

2. Decide what the problem is and how you feel.

3. Think about your choices and their consequences:

    - Ask to join in.
    - Say how you feel, using I-statements.
    - Play with someone else.
    - Do something else that is fun.

4. Decide on your best choice.

5. Do it.

Accepting "No"

1. Stop, take a deep breath, and count to five.

2. Decide what the problem is and how you feel.

3. Think about your choices and their consequences:

   - Say "OK."
   - Say how you feel in a friendly way, using I-statements.
   - Find something else to do.

4. Decide on your best choice.

5. Do it.

Autographs

References

Corey, M.S. & Corey, G. (1992). *Groups: Process and practice* (4th ed.). Pacific Grove, CA: Brooks/Cole.

Doll, B., Sheridan, S.M., & Law, M. (1990). *Friendship group: Parents manual*. Unpublished manual, University of Wisconsin-Madison, Department of Educational Psychology, Madison, WI.

Gresham, F.M. & Elliott, S.N. (1990). *The social skills rating system*. Circle Pines, MN: AGS.

McGinnis, E. & Goldstein, A.P. (1984). *Skillstreaming the elementary school child: A guide for teaching prosocial skills*. Champaign, IL: Research Press.

Merrell, K. (1993). *School social behavior scales*. Eugene, OR: Castalia.

Jenson, W.R., Rhode, G., & Reavis, H.K. (1994). *The tough kid tool box*. Longmont, CO: Sopris West.

Jones, R.N., Sheridan, S.M., & Binns, W.R. (1993). Schoolwide social skills training: Providing preventive services to students at-risk. *School Psychology Quarterly*, *8*, 57-80.

Rhode, G., Jenson, W.R., & Reavis, H.K. (1992). *The tough kid book: Practical classroom management strategies*. Longmont, CO: Sopris West.

Sheridan, S.M., Dee, C.C., Morgan, J.C., McCormick, M.E., & Walker, D. (1996). A multimethod intervention for social skills deficits in children with ADHD and their parents. *School Psychology Review*, *25*, 57-76.

Walker, H.M., Severson, H., Stiller, B., Williams, G., Haring, N., Shinn, M., & Todis, B. (1988). Systematic screening of pupils in the elementary age ranges at risk for behavior disorders: development and trial testing of multiple gating model. *Remedial and Special Education*, *9*(3), 8-20.

Walker, H. & McConnell, S. (1988). *Walker-McConnell Scale of Social Competence*. Austin, TX: Pro-Ed.

Other Materials From the "Tough Kid" Series

The Tough Kid Book
Practical Classroom Management Strategies

Ginger Rhode, William R. Jenson, and
H. Kenton Reavis

If you are preparing to teach—and thus work with "Tough Kids"—*The Tough Kid Book* will be a survival manual for your first years of teaching. If you are a practicing teacher, this is a resource they should have used when you were in college. *The Tough Kid Book* is written for both regular and special education teachers. The research-validated solutions included in this book help to reduce disruptive behavior in Tough Kids without big investments of the teacher's time, money, or emotions. These solutions also provide Tough Kids with behavioral, academic, and social survival skills. This book contains a wealth of ready to use strategies and identifies other commercially available, practical resources for teachers who want even more in-depth assistance. Use *The Tough Kid Book* to make the classroom a pleasant, productive environment for you and your students. Learn to enjoy teaching and Monday mornings again—turn Tough Kids into great kids! 120 pages.

The Tough Kid Tool Box
A collection of classroom tools

William R. Jenson, Ginger Rhode, and H. Kenton Reavis

The Tough Kid Tool Box provides teachers at all grade levels with straightforward, classroom-tested, ready to use materials for managing and motivating tough to teach students. *The Tough Kid Book* readers will recognize such gems as:

- Behavior Observation Forms
- Mystery Motivator Charts
- Reward Spinners
- Icon "Countoons" for Self-Monitoring
- Classroom Contracts
- Reinforcer Lists
- Point Cards
- And Many, Many More
- Classroom Activity Schedules for Maximum Engaged Time

If you have *The Tough Kid Book*, this affordable companion piece is a must for you. Even if you haven't read *The Tough Kid Book*, you will find this resource immediately useful since all of the reproducible tools come with step-by-step instructions. *The Tough Kid Tool Box* is designed for teachers who want to save time but who also want to use effective, positive procedures to manage Tough Kid behavior in their classrooms. 214 pages.

The Tough Kid Video Series
A comprehensive staff development tool

Now the Tough Kid issues facing educators, administrators, and parents have been captured in *The Tough Kid Video Series*, a set of six 50-minute videotape presentations featuring some of the country's most prominent education specialists in at-risk behavior. Each tape offers practical strategies for effectively working with today's Tough Kids:

1. In *Behavior Management: Positive Approaches*, Dr. Bill Jenson offers an overview of Tough Kid behavior, including how to define and assess a Tough Kid, and explains how to increase student motivation.

2. In *Behavior Management: Reductive Techniques*, Drs. Ken Reavis and Ginger Rhode outline effective techniques to increase compliance and reduce Tough Kids' disruptive behaviors.

3. In *Social Skills*, Dr. Hill Walker reviews the extensive research on social skills instruction and provides rules for implementing social skills curricula/ teaching social skills to Tough Kids.

4. In *Instructional Strategies*, Drs. Jim Ysseldyke and Bob Algozzine explain how to effectively teach the Tough Kid using their comprehensive model for instruction, which emphasizes planning, managing, delivering, and evaluating instruction.

5. In *Study Skills*, Dr. Anita Archer explains how teachers can help all students, including Tough Kids, master vital organization and study skills.

6. In *School-Wide Techniques*, Dr. Randy Sprick discusses whole school applications of the Tough Kid techniques, and offers a clear approach to creating a school environment that supports individual student discipline plans.

The Tough Kid Video Series can be used in its entirety as a comprehensive staff development tool, or each individual tape may be used by teachers who need help in specific areas.

SOPRIS
WEST

To order any of the materials in the
"Tough Kid" Series, or for a free Sopris
West Catalog . . .

Call **(800) 547-6747**   or   Visit Our Website: **www.sopriswest.com**